Lifting the Fog of Legalese

Lifting the Fog of Legalese

Essays on Plain Language

Joseph Kimble

CAROLINA ACADEMIC PRESS
Durham, North Carolina

Library of Congress Cataloging-in-Publication Data

Kimble, Joseph.
    Lifting the fog of legalese : essays on plain language /
    by Joseph Kimble.
                p. cm.
    Includes bibliographical references and index.
    ISBN 1-59460-212-3 (alk. paper)
    1. Law—United States—Language. 2. Law—United States—
Terminology. 3. Legal composition. I. Title.

KF250.K54 2006
349.7301'4—dc22   2005028131

Carolina Academic Press
700 Kent Street
Durham, North Carolina 27701
Telephone (919) 489-7486
Fax (919) 493-5668
www.cap-press.com

Printed in the United States of America

For my parents, Ralph and Marjorie Kimble

CONTENTS

List of Before-and-After Examples

PREFACE

I wrote these essays over 15 years. They originally appeared in six publications, including two that I edit: the *Michigan Bar Journal*'s "Plain Language" column (edited since 1988), *The Scribes Journal of Legal Writing* (edited since 2001), *Court Review*, *Business Law Today*, *Trial*, and *Clarity*. When an essay refers to the "column," that means the "Plain Language" column.

Naturally, I've done a little updating and revising, but on the whole, the changes are fairly minor. I did split one essay into two parts to correspond with the two parts of the book.

I realize that I repeat points in some of the essays, and for a reason. I wanted each essay (except for the one that is split up) to remain more or less intact and self-contained, so you could dip into it without having read some other part of the book. At the same time, because the false criticisms of plain language are so persistent and the failings of legalese so recurring, they need to be addressed at every turn with the same arguments, evidence, sources, and remedies. Old thinking and old ways will not easily or quickly loosen their grip. Reformers must be relentless.

∾ ∾ ∾

I'm indebted to three top-notch editors who read this entire book: Joseph Spaniol, the former Clerk of the United States Supreme Court; David Schultz of Jones McClure Publishing; and Karen Magnuson, a copyeditor like no other. We have worked together on other projects, so my debt only mounts.

INTRODUCTION

These essays call on lawyers to face some terrible truths: although lawyers write for a living, most legal writing is bad and has been for centuries; most lawyers recognize this failing from what they read, but still fancy themselves to be rather good writers, thank you; likewise, most lawyers strongly prefer other writers' prose to be plainer, simpler, shorter, clearer, but they also strongly resist changing their own style (that's the great disconnect); every possible rationalization for traditional legal style has been discredited; and the costs of our bad writing and funny talk — the time and money wasted and the public disrespect — are incalculable.

So what's wrong with traditional style? It's a stew of all the worst faults of formal and official prose, seasoned with the peculiar expressions and mannerisms that lawyers perpetuate.

The legal vocabulary is commonly archaic and inflated. It abounds in doublets and triplets (*give, devise, and bequeath*); *here-, there-,* and *where-* words (*herein, thereto*); multiword prepositions (*with regard to, subsequent to*); other wordy phrases (*in the event that, until such time as*); and strange, useless jargon (*said injury; case at bar; inter alia; Further affiant sayeth naught; In witness whereof, the parties hereto have affixed their signatures*).

Legal sentences tend to be long and flabby. They overuse the passive voice and abstract nouns (in place of strong verbs). They often pile up conditions at the beginning of the sentence. They delay the verb by putting lists of items in the subject or by embedding clauses between the main subject and verb. And they tack exceptions onto the end (sometimes in so-called provisos) instead of putting them in a new sentence.

More generally, legal writing tends to be poorly organized and poorly formatted. The information is not broken down into manageable parts and subparts that are logically ordered for the readers and that use headings to guide them. The writing does not make effective use of summaries, vertical lists, examples, tables and charts, and modern techniques for document design. And in its effort to be precise and exhaustive, it becomes excessively detailed and too often sinks into redundancy, ambiguity, and error.

The result is legalese — a form of prose so jumbled, dense, verbose, and overloaded that it confuses and frustrates most everyday readers and even many lawyers.

Of course, this book is full of examples, but let me offer another small assortment to set the stage.

- *From a letter*: Please be advised that I am in receipt of your letter in regard to the above matter and have enclosed my response to the same.

  In other words: I received your letter about the *Spann* case and have enclosed my response.

- *From another letter*: I am herewith returning the stipulation to dismiss in the above entitled matter; the same being duly executed by me.

  In other words: I have signed and enclosed the stipulation to dismiss the *Byrd* case.

- *From a medical arbitration form*: This agreement to arbitrate is not a prerequisite to health care or treatment and may be revoked 60 days after execution by notification in writing.

  In other words: You don't have to sign this to get treatment here. And if you do sign, you can cancel within 60 days after you sign by writing to _____.

- *From a ballot proposal*: Shall the previously voted increase in excess of the limitation on the amount of taxes that may be assessed on all property in the Charter Township of Meridian, Ingham County, Michigan, as reduced by the required millage rollback, which last resulted in a levy of .2947 mills ($0.2947 on each $1,000 of State Equalized Valuation), be renewed for levy in the years 1995 through 2004 inclusive to continue the Township's existing program for engineering, constructing, and maintaining pedestrian/bicycle pathways within the Township, which will raise for the Township in the first year of the levy the estimated sum of $253,000?

In other words: Should Meridian Township continue its property tax of .2947 mills for pedestrian and bike paths? Each year, this would cost you about $15 for each $50,000 of your state equalized valuation. The charge would last from 1995 through 2004. This tax would raise an estimated $253,000 in the first year.

- *From a statute*: In case any building or structure is erected, constructed, reconstructed, altered, converted or maintained, or any building, structure or land is used, or any land is divided into lots, blocks or sites in violation of this article or of any local law, ordinance or other regulation made under authority conferred thereby, the proper local authorities of the town, in addition to other remedies, may institute any appropriate action or proceedings to prevent such unlawful erection, construction, reconstruction, alteration, conversion, maintenance, use or division of land, to restrain, correct or abate such violation, to prevent the occupancy of said building, structure or land or to prevent any illegal act, conduct, business or use in or about such premises.

  In other words: If any use of land or of a structure — or if the structure itself — violates this article or a local law or regulation, the proper town authorities may take legal action to correct or end the violation and to prevent any illegal use of the premises. [Incidentally, does the statute apply to preexisting uses and structures?]

- *From a contract* (a standard provision): If any term, provision, Section, or portion of this Agreement, or the application thereof to any person, place, or circumstance, shall be held to be invalid, void, or unenforceable by a court of competent jurisdiction, the remaining terms, provisions, Sections, and portions of this Agreement shall nevertheless continue in full force and effect without being impaired or invalidated in any way.

In other words: If a court invalidates any portion of this agreement, the rest of it remains in effect.

• *From a mortgage*: The undersigned borrower(s) for and in consideration of The Mortgage Company, this date funding the closing of the above-referenced property, agrees, if requested by Lender or Closing Agent for Lender, to fully cooperate and adjust for clerical errors, any or all loan closing documentation if deemed necessary or desirable in the reasonable discretion of Lender to enable Lender to sell, convey, seek guarantee, or market said loan to any entity, including but not limited to an investor, Federal National Mortgage Association, Federal Home Loan Mortgage Corporation, or the Federal Housing Authority. The undersigned borrower(s) do hereby so agree and covenant in order to assure that the loan documentation executed this date will conform and be acceptable in the market place in the instance of transfer, sale, or conveyance by Lender of its interest in and to said loan documentation.

In other words: If the lender asks us to, we will cooperate in fixing clerical errors in the closing documents so that the loan can be marketed and transferred to someone else.

• *From a motion in a lawsuit*: Now comes Richard Penniman, hereinafter referred to as "Penniman," Third-Party Defendant in the above-styled and numbered action, and files this Motion to Dismiss pursuant to 12(b)(6) of the Federal Rules of Civil Procedure, and in support thereof will respectfully show unto this Court as follows.

In other words: Richard Penniman moves to dismiss under Rule 12(b)(6).

- *From a rule of court procedure*: When an order is made in favor of a person who is not a party to the action, that person may enforce obedience to the order by the same process as if a party; and, when obedience to an order may be lawfully enforced against a person who is not a party, that person is liable to the same process for enforcing obedience to the order as if a party.

  In other words: When an order grants relief for a nonparty or may be enforced against a nonparty, the procedure for enforcing the order is the same as for a party.

- *From a jury instruction*: The fact that the defendant did not testify is not a factor from which any inference unfavorable to the defendant may be drawn.

  In other words: Although Mr. Charles didn't testify, you should not hold that against him. Don't consider it in any way.

Such a mess we lawyers have gotten ourselves into. And because law touches almost everything in some way, so does the fog of legalese. I think no reform would more fundamentally improve our profession and the work we do than learning to express ourselves in plain language. To that end, this book.

PART ONE

Arguments and Evidence

Strike Three for Legalese

In the October 1987 "Plain Language" column, we reported on a survey of Michigan judges and lawyers in which they showed a strong preference for plain English over legalese.[1] The same survey was then done in Florida and Louisiana — with strikingly similar results in favor of plain English. So geography makes no difference: plain English wins everywhere.

The Survey

The survey had its origin in a persistent question from my students: how will judges and lawyers react to the writing style that I was trying to teach? The only way to find out was to test them.

The survey form is shown in the box on the next two pages. The form invited readers to choose the A or B version of six paragraphs — one version in plain English and the other in traditional legal style. Neither the survey form nor the cover letter referred to "plain English" or "legalese." Rather, the cover letter introduced the survey as part of an effort to "test language trends in the legal profession."

---

[1] Steve Harrington & Joseph Kimble, *Survey: Plain English Wins Every Which Way*, 66 Mich. B.J. 1024 (Oct. 1987).

Legal-Language Survey

Below are paragraphs taken from legal documents. Please mark your preference for paragraph A or B in the space provided.

1. _____

   A [ ] Now comes the above named John Smith, plaintiff herein, by and through Darrow & Holmes, his attorneys of record, and shows unto this Honorable Court as follows:

   B [ ] For his complaint, the plaintiff says:

2. _____

   A [ ] I received a completed copy of this note and disclosure statement before I signed the note.

               _____ Date _____

   B [ ] Maker(s) hereby acknowledge receipt of a completely filled in copy of this note and disclosure statement prior to execution hereof this ____ day of _____, 19____.

3. _____

   A [ ] Petitioner's argument that exclusion of the press from the trial and subsequent suppression of the trial transcripts is, in effect, a prior restraint is contrary to the facts.

   B [ ] Petitioner argued that it is a prior restraint to exclude the press from the trial and later suppress the trial transcripts. This argument is contrary to the facts.

4. _____

   A [ ] One test that is helpful in determining whether or not a person was negligent is to ask and answer whether or not, if a person of ordinary prudence had been in the same situation and possessed of the same knowledge, he would have foreseen or anticipated that someone might have been injured by or as a result of his action or inaction. If such a result from certain conduct would be foreseeable by a person of ordinary prudence with like knowledge and in like situation, and if the conduct reasonably could be avoidable, then not to avoid it would be negligence.

B [ ] To decide whether the defendant was negligent, there is a test you can use. Consider how a reasonably careful person would have acted in the same situation. To find the defendant negligent, you would have to answer "yes" to the following two questions:

1) Would a reasonably careful person have realized in advance that someone might be injured by the defendant's conduct?

2) Could a reasonably careful person have avoided behaving as defendant did?

If your answer to both of these questions is "yes," then the defendant was negligent. You can use the same test in deciding whether the plaintiff was negligent.

5. _____

A [ ] The company will pay benefits only if the insured notifies the company of the loss.

B [ ] Payment of benefits will not be made by the company if the insured fails to provide notification of the loss.

6. _____

A [ ] If attorneys want to comment on the proposed change in court procedures, they may send comments in writing to the Clerk, 233 Main St., Gotham City, before Feb. 21, 1987.

B [ ] Interested attorneys may, on or before Feb. 20, 1987, submit to the Clerk, 233 Main St., Gotham City, written comments regarding the proposed change in court procedures.

Each of these six paragraphs was designed to test for specific aspects of plain English.

Paragraph 1

1A uses a wordy, obsolete formalism.
1B is simple and direct.

Paragraph 2

2A uses the first person (*I*) and strong, simple verbs (*received* and *signed*).

2B uses archaic and inflated words (*hereby*, *hereof*, and *prior to*), and it uses abstract nouns (*receipt* and *execution*) instead of the strong verbs.

Paragraph 3

3A is hard to read because of the long, intrusive clause between the subject (*petitioner's argument*) and the predicate (*is contrary to the facts*). And 3A again turns strong verbs into abstract nouns (*argument, exclusion,* and *suppression*).

3B removes the intrusive clause and puts the conclusion in a separate short sentence. 3B also uses stronger verb forms (*argued, to exclude,* and *[to] suppress*) instead of the abstract nouns.

Paragraph 4

4A uses long sentences again and a series of redundant pairs. It also defines "negligence" negatively ("not to avoid [the conduct]").

4B uses shorter sentences. It addresses jurors in the second person (*you*) and walks them through the instruction step by step. 4B also defines "negligence" positively. 4B is no shorter than 4A, but plain writing does not always mean the fewest possible words.

Paragraph 5

5A uses positive form and strong verbs (*will pay* and *notifies*) in the active voice.

5B uses two negatives (*will not be made* and *fails to provide*). It also turns the verbs into nouns (*payment* and *notification*), and the active voice into the passive (*will not be made*).

Paragraph 6

6A uses the familiar and readable *if . . . [then] . . .* construction. It keeps the subjects and verbs together, and it puts the important details at the end. It also uses the simple word *send* instead of *submit*, and the simple *on* instead of *regarding*.

6B has two intrusive phrases: one inside the verb (*may submit*) and one between the verb (*submit*) and its object (*comments*).

As you have gathered, the plain-English answers are 1B, 2A, 3B, 4B, 5A, and 6A. The alternative versions contain many of the familiar enemies of plain English: obsolete formalisms (*Now comes . . .*); archaic words (*hereby, hereof*); longer and less common words (*subsequent, submit*) instead of simple, everyday words (*later, send*); wordy phrases (*above named, prior to*); doublets (*by and through, foreseen or anticipated*); abstract nouns (*execution, payment, notification*) created from strong verbs; passive voice (*payment will not be made*); long sentences; intrusive phrases; and negative form.

The Responses

The original survey, in Michigan, was sent to a random sample of 300 judges and 500 lawyers. Responses came from 425 (53%). The judges preferred plain English in 85% of their responses, and the lawyers in 80%.

The Florida survey was done by Barbara Child, the former director of legal drafting at the University of Florida College of Law. She reported her results in the *Florida Bar Journal*.[2] She surveyed 558 judges and 558 lawyers, and received responses from 628 (56%). The judges preferred plain English in 86% of their responses, the lawyers in 80% — almost identical to the Michigan results.

In her article, Child reviews the trend toward plain English and credits the practicing bar in Michigan with having "taken on plain English reform wholesale."[3] At the same time, she acknowledges the overriding need "for practice to catch up with preference."[4]

The Louisiana survey was done by Joseph Prokop, who was a student at Thomas Cooley Law School. He sent the survey to judges only, 247 judges of the Supreme Court, Court of Appeal, and trial courts. In 123 responses, those judges preferred the plain-English versions 82% of the time.

No doubt about it. Submitted to the judgment of 1,176 law professionals in three states, legalese has struck out.

There is one other study worth mentioning. It focused more narrowly on the persuasive form of legal writing.[5] In California, ten appellate judges and their research attorneys, reading passages from appellate briefs, rated the passages written in legalese as "substantively weaker and less persuasive than the plain English versions."[6]

---

[2] Barbara Child, *Language Preferences of Judges and Lawyers: A Florida Survey*, 64 Fla. B.J. 32 (Feb. 1990).

[3] *Id.* at 34.

[4] *Id.* at 36.

[5] Robert W. Benson & Joan B. Kessler, *Legalese v. Plain English: An Empirical Study of Persuasion and Credibility in Appellate Brief Writing*, 20 Loy. L.A. L. Rev. 301 (1987).

[6] *Id.* at 301.

The Message

When the discussion of legal writing turns to concrete examples, we naturally prefer the greater clarity and readability of plain English. As *readers* we prefer it; that is the message — and the moral imperative — for writers. If we expect the other person's writing to be straightforward, we had better demand it of our own. Remember the Golden Rule.

Unfortunately, the myths about plain English persist, and so does legalese. The myths number at least four.

Myth One: Plain-English advocates want first-grade prose or want to reduce writing to the lowest common denominator. Not true. We advocate writing that is as simple, direct, and economical as the circumstances allow. We have encouraged lawyers to at least get started by doing away with obsolete formalisms, archaic terms, doublets and triplets, and some other common affronts to plain style.[7]

In the 1980s and '90s, the Plain English Committee of Michigan's state bar translated hundreds of passages into plain English and helped revise dozens of forms. And this column has offered examples almost every month since May 1984. Rarely have we heard that the plain-English versions changed the meaning, or were simpleminded, or were inferior to the originals.

Far from advocating first-grade prose, we have said many times that writing plain English only *looks* easy. As Barbara Child points out, "it requires sophistication to produce documents that are consistently coherent, clear, and readable. By contrast, the 'specialized tongue' of lawyers, 'legalese,' may even be easier to write because it relies on convention instead of thought."[8]

---

[7] T. Selden Edgerton (pseudonym for George Hathaway), *The Ten Commandments of How to Not Write in Plain English*, 65 Mich. B.J. 1168 (Nov. 1986); Joseph Kimble, *Protecting Your Writing from Law Practice*, 66 Mich. B.J. 912 (Sept. 1987).

[8] Child, *supra* note 2, at 32.

Myth Two: Plain English does not allow for literary effect or recognize the ceremonial value of legal language. Not true. Plain English has nothing against an attractive writing style; or against a rhetorical flourish or strategy in the right context, such as a persuasive brief; or against *the truth, the whole truth, and nothing but the truth* to convey a sense of gravity in the courtroom. These things are matters of context, judgment, effectiveness, and degree.

The trouble is that the successful and legitimate uses of expressive style have been overwhelmed by legalese. Ask the judges or clerks who read briefs for a living how much literature they see. Ask them whether they would settle for writing that is clear and concise. Or test the literary hypothesis against a random volume from a case reporter.

At any rate, there is little room for literary effect in the neutral style of contracts, wills, consumer forms, and so on. Yet this seems to be where legalese is thickest.

We have no answer for those who find beauty in *Now comes the plaintiff*. But those who enjoy a fresh metaphor or a rhythmic and well-turned sentence can rest assured: in most contexts, these are quite compatible with the goals of plain English. And in every context, simplicity has a beauty of its own.

Myth Three: Plain English is impossible because legal writing includes so many terms of art. This one dies hard. Of course legal writing and analysis may involve terms of art, such as *hearsay* and *res judicata*. Legitimate terms of art convey in a word or two a fairly specific, settled meaning. They are useful when lawyers write for each other, but when we write for a lay audience, terms of art impose a barrier. If we cannot avoid them, we should at least try to explain them.

Terms of art are limited in another, more important way: they are but a small part of any legal paper. One study of a real-estate sales agreement found that only about 3% of the words had significant legal meaning based on precedent.[9] The rest of a legal paper can be written in plain English, without *hereby* or *in consideration of the premises set forth herein* or *Wherefore, plaintiff prays* or *ordered, adjudged, and decreed* or *due to the fact that* or *in the event of default on the part of the buyer*.

The task for legal writers is to separate real terms of art from all the rubble. The one indispensable guide is Bryan Garner's *Dictionary of Modern Legal Usage* (2d ed. 1995).

Myth Four: Plain English is impossible because the law deals with complicated ideas that require great precision. This notion, like the previous one, contains a kernel of truth, but only a kernel.

First, much of what plain English opposes has nothing to do with precision. The word *hereby* does not add an iota of precision. *Said plaintiff* is no more precise than *the plaintiff*. *In the event of default on the part of the buyer* is no more precise than *if the buyer defaults*.

Second, it's no criticism of plain English that many important legal ideas cannot be made precise. The terms *reasonable doubt* and *good cause* and *gross negligence*, for instance, are *inherently* vague. The best we can do with terms like these is to make them as clear and precise as possible.

Third, plain-English principles can usually make even complicated ideas more clear. This column has yet to find a sentence too complex for plain English.[10] Another columnist points out that "[i]f anything, complex ideas cry out for clear, simple, transparent prose. The substance is challenging enough; don't compound the challenge with a difficult prose style."[11] He suggests that we think of plain English as a means to clear writing, a goal we can all agree on.

---

[9] Benson Barr, George Hathaway, Nancy Omichinski & Diana Pratt, *Legalese and the Myth of Case Precedent*, 64 Mich. B.J. 1136, 1137 (Oct. 1985).

[10] George Hathaway, *Results of the "Too Complex for Plain English" Search*, 68 Mich. B.J. 1194 (Dec. 1989).

[11] Mark Mathewson, *Verbatim*, 18 Student Lawyer 12, 13 (Oct. 1989).

Let's abandon these myths. Legalese persists for the same reasons as always — habit, inertia, formbooks, fear of change, and notions of prestige. These reasons are more emotional than intellectual. We may think that clients expect and pay for legalese, but it has prompted endless criticism and ridicule.[12] And besides, since legalese has nothing of substance to recommend it, its dubious prestige value depends on ignorance. We cannot fool people forever. Our main goal should be to communicate, not to impress.

Legalese persists for another, less obvious reason — one that goes more to training and skill. Law schools have neglected legal drafting. Most first-year writing courses concentrate on research, analysis, and advocacy; students write office memorandums and appellate briefs. Law schools have been much slower to offer courses in drafting contracts, wills, legislation, and the like. The result: "Many lawyers now in practice have had no formal training in the fundamental principles of drafting such documents, much less techniques to make them readable."[13]

Contracts, real-estate documents, wills and trusts, powers of attorney, consumer forms, administrative rules, legislation — this is the realm of drafting, where legalese is thickest and the need for reform is greatest.

---

[12] *See* Appendix 1 to this book.
[13] Child, *supra* note 2, at 36.

∽ ∽ ∽

After this article was written, the same survey was conducted among judges in Texas. Here are the collected results.

	Surveys Returned	Percentage Returned	Percentage of Responses Favoring Plain Language	
			Judges	Lawyers
Michigan	425	53%	85%	80%
Florida	628	56%	86%	80%
Louisiana	123	50%	82%	—
Texas	286	60%	82%	—

The Straight Skinny on
Better Judicial Opinions
(Part 1)

May it please the court: this article presents the first empirical testing of judicial opinions. Of course, you will find no end of commentary on writing opinions — and several books.[1] So we have lots of sensible advice based on perception, experience, judgment, and a feel for good style. But as far as I know, no one has ever tested opinions on readers to see what works and what doesn't.

You will probably not be surprised by the results or by the recommendations for writing effective opinions. Nothing in here will be radically new. My testing confirms what judges and lawyers should have long known but don't regularly practice: if you care to write better opinions (or letters or memos or briefs), then make them straightforward and lean.

Method of Testing

The method was simple: ask lawyers to read two versions of the same opinion, decide which one they like better, and give the reasons why.

---

[1] Ruggero J. Aldisert, *Opinion Writing* (1990); Appellate Judges Conference, American Bar Assn., *Judicial Opinion Writing Manual* (1991); Joyce J. George, *Judicial Opinion Writing Handbook* (4th ed. 2000); Robert A. Leflar, *Appellate Judicial Opinions* (1974); *see also* Federal Judicial Center, *Judicial Writing Manual* (1991).

So I started by taking a volume of the *Michigan Appeals Reports* from the shelf, and I spent maybe 10 or 15 minutes picking an opinion. I had only three criteria. First, it had to be fairly short so that readers would take the time to read the two versions. Second, it had to deal with an uncontroversial subject. I picked a case involving insurance coverage. Pretty bland, but I did not want readers to be distracted by impressions of how the case should have been decided. Third, the writing had to be fairly typical. I did not try to find a case that I thought was quite badly written. Of course, that would have skewed the results, and readers and reviewers would have seen through that game easily enough. You can be the judge of whether the writing in the opinion seems about average for most of the opinions you read.

The case is *Wills v. State Farm Insurance Co.*[2] It seems that Robert Wills was driving along one day, minding his own business, when another car pulled alongside him in the passing lane, fired shots toward his car, and kept right on cruising down the road, never to be seen again. Wills wanted to collect uninsured-motorist benefits. To collect under his policy, he needed to show that the other car had "struck" his car.

I revised the published opinion, did pilot-testing on third-year law students, and then randomly mailed the original and revised versions to 700 Michigan lawyers. Actually, I sent them out in two mailings and tinkered a little with the revised opinion between mailings. But the tinkering made almost no difference in the results. I labeled one opinion O (my own clever code for "original") and the other opinion X (first mailing) or Y (second mailing). For simplicity, I'll just call the revised opinion the Y opinion.

I had someone else sign the cover letter, since Michigan lawyers might recognize me as the editor of the "Plain Language" column in the *Michigan Bar Journal.* Along with the cover letter and two opinions, I included a one-page

---

[2]   564 N.W.2d 488 (Mich. App. 1997).

sheet called "Questions About the Opinions." Readers were asked which opinion they liked better, how they rated the two opinions on a 1-to-10 scale, and the top two reasons why they liked the one better than the other.

Readers who liked the O version better had these reasons to choose from:

- It's more traditional.
- It's better organized.
- It cites more cases, so it will be more helpful for research.
- The other opinion leaves out important details.
- Other reason: _____

_____

Readers who liked the Y version better had these reasons to choose from:

- It has a summary at the beginning.
- It uses headings.
- It's better organized.
- It leaves out a lot of unnecessary detail.
- Other reason: _____

_____

I tried hard to identify what I thought the most likely reasons would be and to state them dispassionately. I also asked trusted colleagues to look them over.

In Appendix A (page 23), you'll find the complete package that readers received. There was just one variable. I thought that it might make a difference which opinion the readers looked over first, so in half the packages the O opinion appeared first, and in the other half the Y opinion appeared first. If the O opinion came first (as it does in Appendix A), then the O opinion came first in the choices on the "Questions" page. (See page 35.) And I just reversed it if the Y opinion came first.

Of the 700 lawyers who received the package, 251 responded by returning the "Questions" page. I considered that a good response, since they had to read seven pages of opinions (ten pages in this book's format) and then answer the questions.

The results, as I said, were no surprise: readers strongly preferred the revised version. I'll dissect the results in a moment, but first let me put them alongside some other testing of legal and official writing.

Previous Studies — Mine and Others'

This testing of opinions was my fourth round of testing.

First, a colleague and I prepared a study that was eventually conducted in four states. We asked readers to check off their preference for the A or B version of six different paragraphs from various legal documents. One version of each paragraph was in plain language and the other in traditional legal style — although they were not identified that way, but only as A and B. Altogether, 1,462 judges and lawyers responded, and in all four states they preferred the plain-language versions by margins running from 80% to 86%.[3]

Second, I tested a contract used by a Michigan state agency. I tested it on the agency staff and on law students. Half got the original contract, half got the plain-language version, and they all got the same questions to answer. The agency staff was 45% more accurate and 16% faster using the plain-language version. The law students were 23% more accurate and 20% faster.[4]

Third, I tested a South African statute that two colleagues and I had redrafted as part of a demonstration project for that country's new Ministry of Justice. I tested it on law

---

[3] *Strike Three for Legalese*, this book at 3, 13.

[4] *Answering the Critics of Plain Language*, 5 Scribes J. Legal Writing 51, 69–70, 83–85 (1994–1995).

students and on a law-school staff. The law students were 17% more accurate and 5% faster using the redrafted version, and they rated it 41% easier to use. The law-school staff was 21% more accurate and 9% faster, and they rated it 26% easier to use.[5]

I summarized these three studies — along with dozens more — in *Answering the Critics of Plain Language* and *Writing for Dollars, Writing to Please*, which appeared in Volumes 5 and 6 of *The Scribes Journal of Legal Writing*. Once and for all, the weight of all these studies should put to rest the terrible, stubborn myths about plain language — that it dumbs down the language, that it involves a few limited guidelines (use short sentences, the active voice, and simple words), that legal readers won't like it, that it's not accurate or precise, that it's a matter of personal style and does not entail any larger public benefit, and that there's no evidence it works. Here's what I said at the end of *Writing for Dollars, Writing to Please*: "There is now compelling evidence that plain language saves money and pleases readers: it is much more likely to be read and understood and heeded — in much less time. It could even help to restore faith in public institutions."[6]

Results of the Opinion-Testing

Out of the 251 lawyers who responded to my mailing, 98, or 39%, preferred the original opinion; 153, or 61%, preferred the revised opinion.

Readers rated the original opinion at an average of 6 on a 1-to-10 scale; they rated the revised opinion at 7. Given the strong preference for the revised opinion, I was a little surprised at those two numbers. Then again, the number for the original opinion seems to confirm that I succeeded in choosing one that's about par for the course. Also, because

---

[5] *Id.* at 69, 71.
[6] 6 Scribes J. Legal Writing 1, 37 (1996–1997).

I was concerned about the amount of reading required, I shortened the original opinion by omitting 500 words of unnecessary detail even before I sent it out. So readers were already seeing a somewhat improved version of the original.

Finally, readers were asked to mark the top two reasons for their preference. Those results appear below. Each number shows how many readers marked that reason as their first or second reason. (The numbers do not add up perfectly because some readers did not follow the instructions.) For readers who liked the O (original) opinion better:

It's more traditional.   9

It's better organized.   52

It cites more cases, so it will be more   53
    helpful for research.

The other opinion leaves out important details.   43

Other reason: better analysis   34
    (most common "other reason").

For readers who liked the Y (revised) opinion better:

It has a summary at the beginning.   77

It uses headings.   37

It's better organized.   72

It leaves out a lot of unnecessary detail.   84

Other reasons: clearer, easier to read,   34
    more succinct, in plain English,
    not so much legalese.

Although both of these distributions are fairly even, two things seem noteworthy. First and foremost, readers who preferred the revised opinion gave the greatest weight to leaving out unnecessary detail. And since that reason overlapped with many of the "other reasons" those readers gave (more succinct, in plain English, and so on), the exceptional importance of conciseness becomes even more exceptional.[7] Second, readers greatly value a good summary at the beginning of an opinion, and judges should take pains to provide one. Let's hope these two lessons, at least, are reflected in every opinion from now on. That would be almost revolutionary.

ง ง ง

I examine the differences between the original and revised opinions in Part 2, this book at 89.

---

[7] *See* Kristen K. Robbins, *The Inside Scoop: What Federal Judges Really Think About the Way Lawyers Write*, 8 Legal Writing: J. Legal Writing Inst. 257, 279 (2002) (noting, in a survey of federal judges about lawyers' briefs, a "strong, recurring, and unmistakable cry for conciseness and clarity" — qualities that judges ought to strive for in their own writing as well).

Appendix A
The Package That Readers Received

Elisha Jones
964 Briarwick Drive
East Lansing, Michigan 48823

March 18, 1999

Mrs. XXXXXX
XXXXXXXXX
XXXXXXXXX

Dear Mrs. X:

I am a recent law-school graduate who is working on a study of judicial opinions. I believe that no one has ever done a study like this. But I need your help.

I'm trying to determine what lawyers like and dislike about judicial opinions. Obviously, I can't test everything, but I'm trying to test a few things. I'm sending the study to a random selection of Michigan lawyers. The effort has taken a good deal of time and money. I hope you will help me make it worthwhile. I plan to publish the results in the *Michigan Bar Journal*.

Would you please take a few minutes from your busy schedule to read these two short opinions? After you read the two opinions, please answer the questions on the yellow sheet. Then return the yellow sheet to me in the enclosed self-addressed, stamped envelope. Because this study is based on a random sampling, it's crucial to receive your response in order to obtain reliable data.

Thanks very much for your help.

Sincerely,

Elisha Jones

Elisha Jones

STATE OF MICHIGAN

COURT OF APPEALS

Robert Wills

   Plaintiff-Appellee,

v.

State Farm Insurance Company

   Defendant-Appellant.

Before: Judges A, B, and C.

JUDGE A

Plaintiff Robert Wills filed a declaratory judgment action against defendant State Farm Insurance Company to determine whether defendant has a duty to pay benefits under the uninsured motorist provisions found in plaintiff's policy with defendant. Pursuant to the parties' stipulated statement of facts, the trial court granted summary disposition in plaintiff's favor upon finding coverage where gunshots fired from an unidentified automobile passing plaintiff's vehicle caused plaintiff to drive off the road and suffer injuries. Defendant appeals as of right. We reverse and remand.

In 1994, defendant issued a policy of insurance to plaintiff to cover his 1989 Mercury Sable. As part of this policy, defendant promised to pay plaintiff certain damages if he were injured as the result of an automobile accident between his vehicle and a vehicle driven by an uninsured motorist. The policy stated as follows:

> We will pay damages for *bodily injury* an *insured* is legally entitled to collect from the owner or driver of an *uninsured motor vehicle*. The *bodily injury* must be caused by [an] accident arising out of the operation, maintenance or use of an *uninsured motor vehicle*.
>
> *Uninsured Motor Vehicle* — means:
>
>   * * *
>
> 2. a "hit-and-run" land motor vehicle whose owner or driver remains unknown and which strikes
> a. the *insured* or
> b. the vehicle the *insured* is *occupying* and causes *bodily injury* to the *insured*. [Emphasis in original.]

While plaintiff was driving his Sable on Shaw Lake Road in Barry County, another vehicle pulled alongside his car as if it were passing him in the left lane. Suddenly, plaintiff saw a flash and heard gunshots. Reacting to the shots, plaintiff ducked down to the right toward the floor of the passenger area to avoid injury. Upon doing so, plaintiff turned the Sable's steering wheel to the right. The vehicle swerved off the road and hit two trees. As a result of the accident, plaintiff injured his neck and back, requiring surgery. The parties agree that there was no actual physical contact between the unidentified automobile from which the shots were fired and plaintiff's automobile. The unidentified vehicle and its occupants left the scene of the accident, and the identities of the occupants remain unknown.

Plaintiff subsequently filed a claim with defendant for medical and uninsured motorist benefits. Defendant paid plaintiff his medical benefits but denied plaintiff's claim for uninsured motorist benefits because there was no physical contact between plaintiff's Sable and the unidentified vehicle. Plaintiff responded by filing a declaratory judgment action asking the trial court to enter judgment in his favor with regard to the coverage dispute.

Defendant moved for summary disposition under MCR 2.116(C)(8) and (C)(10). At the hearing on defendant's motion, the trial court distinguished this Court's decision in *Kreager v State Farm Mutual Automobile Ins Co*, 197 Mich App 577; 496 NW2d 346 (1992), from the instant case and relied upon *Hill v Citizens Ins Co of America*, 157 Mich App 383; 403 NW2d 147 (1987), to find that a sufficient physical nexus existed between the two involved automobiles because, while they were moving, a projectile came from one car and entered the other. Therefore, the court found in favor of plaintiff under MCR 2.116(C)(8) and (C)(10) and denied defendant's motion.

We review de novo the trial court's rulings with regard to summary disposition motions, declaratory judgments, and questions of law. See *Cardinal Mooney High School v Michigan High School Athletic Ass'n*, 437 Mich 75, 80; 467 NW2d 21 (1991); *State Treasurer v Schuster*, 215 Mich App 347, 350; 547 NW2d 332 (1996); *Michigan Residential Care Ass'n v Dep't of Social Services*, 207 Mich App 373, 375; 526 NW2d 9 (1994).

Uninsured motorist coverage is not required by statute; thus, the contract of insurance determines under what circumstances the benefits will be awarded. *Berry v State Farm Mutual Automobile Ins Co*, 219 Mich App 340, 346; 556 NW2d 207 (1996); *Auto-Owners Ins Co v Harvey*, 219 Mich App 466, 470; 556 NW2d 517 (1996). An uninsured motorist policy's requirement of "physical contact" between a hit-and-run vehicle and the insured or the insured's vehicle is enforceable in Michigan. *Berry, supra* at 347; *Kreager, supra* at 581–583; *Hill, supra* at 394. This Court has construed the physical contact requirement broadly to include indirect physical contact as long as a substantial physical nexus exists between the unidentified vehicle and the object cast off by that vehicle or the object that strikes the insured's vehicle. *Id.*

A "substantial physical nexus" between the unidentified vehicle and the object causing the injury to the insured has been found where the object in question was a *piece* of, or *projected* by, the unidentified vehicle, but not where the object originates from an occupant of an unidentified vehicle. See *Berry, supra* at 350; *Kreager, supra* at 579; *Adams v Zajac*, 110 Mich App 522, 526–527; 313 NW2d 347 (1981). In *Kreager, supra*, an occupant of an unidentified vehicle shot the insured while he stood outside the driver's side of his vehicle. He was standing there because someone in the unidentified vehicle had thrown a bottle at his car, and he responded by throwing the bottle back at the unidentified vehicle. The shooting occurred in apparent retaliation. After determining that the "physical contact" requirement was dispositive of the dispute between the insured and his uninsured motorist insurance carrier, this Court stated:

> Plaintiff's injuries lack a sufficient "physical nexus" with the unidentified vehicle. Unlike the plaintiff in *Hill, supra*, plaintiff was not injured by an object accidentally projected by the uninsured vehicle. Rather, the "projectile" involved [here] was a bullet fired from the handgun used by the assailant. There was no projection resulting from the vehicle itself. [*Kreager, supra* at 583.]

This Court found no "substantial physical nexus" between the insured or his vehicle and the unidentified vehicle. It also agreed with defendant that the insured's injuries did not arise from any physical contact between the vehicles. Thus, in *Kreager, supra* at 582–583, this Court held that the insured could not recover uninsured motorist benefits.

In *Hill, supra* at 384–385, the plaintiff's husband was driving his vehicle when a camper-truck passing in the opposite direction propelled a large rock through the car's windshield, causing the husband's death. Upon reviewing various Michigan and out-of-state cases, this Court found that direct physical contact between the uninsured vehicle and the insured was not required in order to find coverage. *Id.* at 390. Rather, because the parties agreed that a rock came through the windshield just as the other vehicle passed, the plaintiff could "establish a substantial physical nexus between the disappearing vehicle and the object cast off or struck." *Id.* at 394. Moreover, this Court believed that requiring an insured to prove indirect contact would also foreclose the possibility of fraudulent phantom vehicle claims. *Id.* "In summary, the overwhelming majority of jurisdictions hold that the 'physical contact' provision in uninsured motor vehicle coverage may be satisfied even though there is no direct contact between the disappearing vehicle and claimant or claimant's vehicle." *Id.*; see also *Berry, supra* at 347–348, 350.

In the case at bar, the parties stipulated that there was no actual physical contact between plaintiff's automobile and the unidentified vehicle in question. Rather, the bullets fired by an occupant of the unidentified vehicle struck plaintiff's car. Thus, unlike *Hill*, there was no physical contact between the involved vehicles and no projectile that the unidentified vehicle cast against plaintiff's car. See also *Berry, supra* at 343–350 (scrap metal left in road after trailer full of scrap passed through area fifteen minutes before insured collided with it satisfied substantial physical nexus requirement); *Adams, supra* at 526–527 (summary disposition for Secretary of State reversed where insured's vehicle went out of control after striking or swerving to avoid striking a truck tire and rim assembly left in the highway as the indirect physical contact between the involved vehicles was sufficient); *Lord v Auto-Owners Ins Co*, 22 Mich App 669, 672; 177 NW2d 653 (1970) (recovery permitted where a hit-and-run vehicle struck a second vehicle that in turn was propelled into the plaintiff's vehicle). Indeed, as this Court recognized in *Kreager, supra* at 581, the shooting was not related to the assailant's use of a motor vehicle as a motor vehicle because "the shots could just as readily have been fired from a building, a parked car, a bicycle, or by a pedestrian." Thus, where it is undisputed that an *occupant* of an unidentified vehicle moving alongside plaintiff's vehicle shot at and hit plaintiff's vehicle, i.e., the projectile here came from a gun, not from the vehicle itself, plaintiff cannot show the requisite substantial physical nexus between the unidentified vehicle and himself or his vehicle. *Kreager, supra.*

Reversed and remanded for entry of summary disposition in favor of defendant. Defendant, being the prevailing party, may tax costs pursuant to MCR 7.219.

Y

STATE OF MICHIGAN

COURT OF APPEALS

Robert Wills

     Plaintiff-Appellee,

v.

State Farm Insurance Company

     Defendant-Appellant.

Before: Judges A, B, and C.

JUDGE A

Summary

Robert Wills was injured when someone drove by him and fired shots toward his car, causing him to swerve into a tree. He filed a declaratory-judgment action to determine whether State Farm had to pay him uninsured-motorist benefits. The issue is whether there was a "substantial physical nexus" between the unidentified car and Wills's car. The trial court answered yes and granted a summary disposition for Wills. We disagree and reverse. We do not find a substantial physical nexus between the two cars, because the bullets were not projected by the unidentified car itself.

Facts and Procedural History

State Farm's policy promised to pay Wills if he was injured in an accident between his vehicle and an uninsured motor vehicle. The policy defines "uninsured motor vehicle" to include a hit-and-run vehicle that "strikes" Wills's vehicle:

> We will pay damages for bodily injury an insured is legally entitled to collect from the owner or driver of an uninsured motor vehicle. The bodily injury must be caused by [an] accident arising out of the operation, maintenance or use of an uninsured motor vehicle.
>
> *Uninsured Motor Vehicle* — means:
>
> *   *   *
>
> 2. a "hit-and-run" land motor vehicle whose owner or
>   driver remains unknown and *which strikes*
>   a. the insured or
>   b. the *vehicle the insured is occupying* and causes
>   bodily injury to the insured. [Emphasis added.]

As Wills was driving his car in Barry County, another car pulled alongside him in the passing lane. Suddenly, he saw a flash and heard gunshots. Reacting to the shots, he ducked down to the right, pulled the steering wheel to the right, swerved off the road into two trees, and injured himself. There was no actual physical contact — no direct contact — between the two cars. The other car drove away, and its occupants are unknown.

State Farm denied Wills's claim for uninsured-motorist benefits because there was no physical contact between the two cars. Wills filed a declaratory-judgment action, and State Farm moved for summary disposition under MCR 2.116(C)(8) and (C)(10).

The trial court denied State Farm's motion and instead granted a summary disposition for Wills. The court relied on *Hill v Citizens Ins Co*, 157 Mich App 383; 403 NW2d

147 (1987), to find a sufficient physical nexus between the two cars because, while they were moving, a projectile came from one car and entered the other.

We review de novo a ruling on a motion for summary disposition. *State Treasurer v Schuster*, 215 Mich App 347, 350; 547 NW2d 332 (1996).

Analysis of "Substantial Physical Nexus"

Under State Farm's policy, Wills must show that the other car "struck" his car, at least indirectly. In cases involving indirect physical contact, this court has required a "substantial physical nexus" between the unidentified vehicle and the object that it casts off or the object that strikes the policyholder's vehicle. But there is no physical nexus when the striking object comes from an occupant of the unidentified vehicle — as it did here.

The controlling case is *Kreager v State Farm Mutual Automobile Ins Co*, 197 Mich App 577; 496 NW2d 346 (1992). The *Kreager* court distinguished between an object that comes from an occupant and an object that is projected by the unidentified vehicle itself. In *Kreager*, someone in the unidentified vehicle shot the policyholder while he stood outside his car. The court acknowledged that "physical contact" between two vehicles could include indirect physical contact as long as there was "a substantial physical nexus between the disappearing vehicle and the object cast off or struck." *Kreager* at 582 (quoting an earlier case). But the policyholder could not show this physical nexus:

> [P]laintiff was not injured by an object accidentally projected by the uninsured vehicle. Rather, the "projectile" involved was a bullet fired from the handgun used by the assailant. There was no projection resulting from the vehicle itself. [*Kreager* at 583.]

Thus, the injury did not arise out of the use of the unidentified vehicle as a motor vehicle; the assailant could just as well have fired from a bicycle or while on foot.

Furthermore, the case that the trial court relied on, *Hill*, *supra*, is distinguishable. In *Hill*, the unidentified vehicle threw a rock through the policyholder's windshield. So the striking object *was* projected by the vehicle itself. See also *Berry v State Farm Mutual Automobile Ins Co*, 219 Mich App 340; 566 NW2d 207 (1996) (finding a substantial physical nexus between a disappearing truck full of scrap metal and a piece of metal left in the road).

The present case is like *Kreager*, not *Hill*: the projectile came from a gun fired by an occupant of the unidentified vehicle, not from the vehicle itself. Because Wills cannot show a substantial physical nexus between the uninsured vehicle and his vehicle, he is not entitled to benefits.

We reverse and remand for the entry of summary disposition in favor of defendant. Defendant, as the prevailing party, may tax costs under MCR 7.219.

Questions About the Opinions

1. You read two opinions, O and Y. Which one did you like better? Please put a check mark next to the one you liked better.

   ☐ O   ☐ Y

2. On a scale of 1 (very poor) to 10 (very good), how do you rate the two opinions?

   ___ O   ___ Y

3. If you liked O better, please give the top two reasons why you liked O better. Mark 1 next to your top reason, and mark 2 next to your second top reason.

   ____ It's more traditional.

   ____ It's better organized.

   ____ It cites more cases, so it will be more helpful for research.

   ____ The other opinion leaves out important details.

   ____ Other reason: _____

   _____

   OR

   If you liked Y better, please give the top two reasons why you liked Y better. Mark 1 next to your top reason, and mark 2 next to your second top reason.

   ____ It has a summary at the beginning.

   ____ It uses headings.

   ____ It's better organized.

   ____ It leaves out a lot of unnecessary detail.

   ____ Other reason: _____

   _____

The Great Myth That
Plain Language Is Not Precise

Occasionally, when you try to convert from legalese to plain language, someone will come forward and assert that you made a mistake. You missed something in the translation. You inadvertently changed the substance.

Never mind that translating legalese — like translating a foreign language — is no easy matter. Never mind that, despite the difficulties, good writers have successfully revised countless legal documents into plain — or plainer — language. Never mind that many of these documents have involved tough subjects like financial disclosure, corporate takeovers, and disability insurance, not to mention jury instructions, the Federal Rules of Civil, Criminal, and Appellate Procedure, Article 9 of the Uniform Commercial Code, and various federal regulations issued after President Clinton's memorandum on plain language.[1] Never mind that for every inadvertent change, you could probably identify

---

[1] *See* Div. of Corp. Finance, U.S. Sec. & Exch. Commn., *Before & After Plain English Examples and Sample Analyses* (1998); Law Reform Commn. of Victoria, *Plain English and the Law* app. 2, *Plain English Rewrite — Takeovers Code* (1987); David St. L. Kelly & Christopher J. Balmford, Life Ins. Fedn. of Australia, *Simplifying Disability Income Insurance Documents* (1994); Judicial Council of California, *Civil Jury Instructions* (2005 ed.) (available at http://www.courtinfo.ca.gov/ reference/documents/civiljuryinst.pdf); Comm. on Rules of Practice and Procedure, *Preliminary Draft of Proposed Style Revision of the Federal Rules of Civil Procedure* (Feb. 2005) (available at http:// www.uscourts.gov/rules/Prelim_draft_proposed_pt1.pdf); Bryan A. Garner, *The Substance of Style in Federal Rules*, Clarity No. 42, at 15

several ambiguities or uncertainties in the original document. Never mind that the revised document will almost
certainly be better — clearer and more accurate — than the
original. The fact remains that revising and clarifying a legal
document always involves some judgment and some risk.

But the risk is worth it, and writers should not be
dissuaded. Otherwise, the legal profession will never start
to level the mountain of bad forms and models that we have
created. We'll be stuck with the enormous inefficiencies of
traditional style and the frustration it causes.[2] Change is
hard, but change has to come.

Let me offer what I think is a perfect object lesson — a
little story from Michigan.

The Story in Brief

The *Michigan Bar Journal* has a long-standing column called
"Plain Language," which I happen to edit. In the October
1999 column, an experienced corporate attorney, David
Daly, wrote an article called "Taming the Contract Clause
from Hell."[3] Daly undertook to straighten out a mutual-
indemnification clause, one in which each party indemnifies
the other. (I'll give you the full clause in a minute.) Another

---

(*footnote 1 continued*)

(Sept. 1998); Steven O. Weise, *Plain English Comes to the Uniform
Commercial Code*, Clarity No. 42, at 20 (Sept. 1998); *Airworthiness
Directives*, 14 C.F.R. pt. 39 (2004); *Leasing of Solid Minerals Other
Than Coal and Oil Share*, 43 C.F.R. pt. 3500 (2004). For the Clinton
memorandum, see 6 Scribes J. Legal Writing 39 (1996–1997).

[2] *See Answering the Critics of Plain Language*, 5 Scribes J. Legal Writing
51, 62–65, 69–71 (1994–1995) (citing 15 studies showing that plain
language improves readers' comprehension of legal documents); *Writing
for Dollars, Writing to Please*, 6 Scribes J. Legal Writing 1, 7–31 (1996–
1997) (summarizing 25 studies showing that plain language saves time
and money and is strongly preferred by readers).

[3] *Taming the Contract Clause from Hell: A Case Study*, 78 Mich. B.J.
1155 (Oct. 1999).

attorney then wrote a letter to the editor of the *Bar Journal*;[4] the letter pointed to three possible "errors" in Daly's revised version.

First, the revised version said that if the indemnified party is sued and the indemnifying party assumes the defense, the indemnifying party "may select counsel satisfactory to the other party." The original clause said that "the indemnifying party shall be entitled . . . to assume the defense thereof with counsel satisfactory to such indemnified party." Hmm . . . not much difference. But presumably the intended sense is that the counsel *must* be satisfactory to the other party. That could have been made clearer in both versions.

Second, the revised version did not say that until assuming the defense, the indemnifying party must pay the indemnified party's legal fees. The original said: "after notice . . . to assume the defense thereof, the indemnifying party shall not be liable to such indemnified party . . . for any fees of other counsel or any other expenses, in each case subsequently incurred by such indemnified party . . . ." Now, what does that mean — "in each case subsequently incurred"? (And why the comma after *expenses*?) Omit *in each case* and you'll probably get the intended meaning. So that dividing point, when the indemnifying party assumes the defense, should have been explicitly stated in the revised version.

Third, the original clause said that after assuming the defense, "the indemnifying party shall have no liability with respect to any compromise or settlement thereof effected without its consent." Without going into the reasons why, Daly dropped that provision as implicit in assuming the defense; and he added a comparable provision for the *indemnified* party. He might have explained the change. (A

---

4   Published in "Opinion & Dissent," 79 Mich. B.J. 150 (Feb. 2000) (letter originally dated November 1999, when I first saw it and wrote this article).

half-decent editor would have noticed and queried, but I didn't.)

Although these three points in the letter to the *Bar Journal* cannot really be counted as errors, the points were well taken. The troubling part of the letter, though, was this sentence: "As written, the turgid, repetitive and (nearly) unreadable original has a paramount advantage over the concise, clearer version: it gets the intended legal relations right." I hope no one will make too much of statements like this. Please don't conclude that a legal writer has to choose between precision and plain language — that legalese has the advantage of being more precise, and plain language is less likely to get the substance right. That's just not true. In fact, it's the biggest myth of all.

A Look at the Original Clause

Let's back up and review this wondrous clause. (The lines are numbered so that I can refer to them later.)

---

8. Indemnification

. . .

1	(c) Promptly after receipt by an indemnified party under
2	Section 1(g), 8(a) or 8(b) hereof of notice of the commence-
3	ment of any action, such indemnified party shall, if a claim
4	in respect thereto is to be made against an indemnifying
5	party under such Section, give notice to the indemnifying
6	party of the commencement thereof, but the failure so to
7	notify the indemnifying party shall not relieve it of any
8	liability that it may have to any indemnified party except
9	to the extent the indemnifying party demonstrates that the
10	defense of such action is prejudiced thereby. If any such
11	action shall be brought against an indemnified party and it
12	shall give notice to the indemnifying party of the com-
13	mencement thereof, the indemnifying party shall be
14	entitled to participate therein and, to the extent that it shall
15	wish, to assume the defense thereof with counsel satisfac-
16	tory to such indemnified party and, after notice from the

> *(original clause continued)*
>
> 17   indemnifying party to such indemnified party of its
> 18   election so to assume the defense thereof, the indemnifying
> 19   party shall not be liable to such indemnified party under
> 20   such Section for any fees of other counsel or any other
> 21   expenses, in each case subsequently incurred by such
> 22   indemnified party in connection with the defense thereof,
> 23   other than reasonable costs of investigation. If an indem-
> 24   nifying party assumes the defense of such an action, (i) no
> 25   compromise or settlement thereof may be effected by the
> 26   indemnifying party without the indemnified party's
> 27   consent (which shall not be unreasonably withheld) and (ii)
> 28   the indemnifying party shall have no liability with respect
> 29   to any compromise or settlement thereof effected without
> 30   its consent (which shall not be unreasonably withheld). If
> 31   notice is given to an indemnifying party of the commence-
> 32   ment of any action and it does not, within ten days after the
> 33   indemnified party's notice is given, give notice to the
> 34   indemnified party of its election to assume the defense
> 35   thereof, the indemnifying party shall be bound by any
> 36   determination made in such action or any compromise or
> 37   settlement thereof effected by the indemnified party.

In his article, David Daly summarized why this thing is so poorly drafted:

- The sentences don't begin with the main, or independent, clause.
- The sentences are too long.
- It uses too many words.
- It fails to break the material down into subparts.

True enough, but there's more. For all its supposed accuracy and precision, the clause is full of little holes that the dense surface hides.

One: *shall* is misused throughout. Lawyers are uneducable on *shall*, and we should give it up. Commentators and experts agree that it should be used to impose a duty.[5] It means "has a duty to." Essentially, if you can substitute *must*, then the *shall* is correct. So why not just use *must* to begin with?

At any rate, 8 of the 11 *shall*s in the indemnification clause are misused: the verb should be in the present tense. In lines 13–14, for instance, it should be *is entitled*. Luckily, none of the misuses creates an ambiguity, but our professional mishandling of *shall* betrays us in more serious, problematic ways. You can see for yourself by checking *Words and Phrases* — 104 pages and over 1,300 cases dealing with *shall*.

Two: in line 4, what does *thereto* refer to? The action? One of the sections? This typifies the pseudo-precision of our beloved antique jargon — words like *thereto* and *herein* and *such*.

Three: in lines 5 and 20, what does *such Section* refer to? Does it refer to one section in particular or to any one of the three sections?

Four: lines 11–14 seem to say that the indemnifying party may participate in the defense only if the indemnified party gives notice. But why should that right depend on whether notice is given?

Five: in line 14, the *and* should be *or*, right? That is, the indemnifying party can participate in the defense without assuming the defense.

Six: lines 13–15 say that "the indemnifying party shall be entitled . . . , to the extent that it shall wish, to assume the defense thereof . . . ." Does this mean that the indemnifying party may somehow assume part, but not all, of the defense?

---

[5] Barbara Child, *Drafting Legal Documents* 204–06, 383–84 (2d ed. 1992); Reed Dickerson, *The Fundamentals of Legal Drafting* §§ 6.7, 9.4 (2d ed. 1986); Bryan A. Garner, *A Dictionary of Modern Legal Usage* 940 (2d ed. 1995).

Seven: in line 21, the *in each case subsequently incurred* should be *in this case*, right? Better yet, omit *in each case*.

Eight: in lines 25, 29, and 36–37, what's the difference between "compromise" and "settlement"? Is this just another legal doublet, like *null and void*? Or do you need both terms?[6]

Nine: lines 32–33 say "within ten days after the indemnified party's notice [of the action] is given." Shouldn't that be ten days after notice is *received*?

Ten: lines 30–37 set a practical limit of ten days on giving notice to assume the defense. Is there any time limit on when the indemnifying party can decide to *participate* in the defense? Apparently not.

There may be more questions, but that's enough to bring home the point: when you redraft in plain language, you inevitably uncover gaps and uncertainties in legalistic writing. The fog lifts, the drizzle ends, and the light shines through. So I believe that plain language, far from being imprecise, is usually *more* precise than traditional legal style. The imprecisions of legalese are just harder to spot.

Another Revised Version

David Daly's improved plain-language version of the indemnification clause can easily be tweaked to take into account the comments in the letter to the editor. You could do it like this:

---

[6] *See* Garner, *supra* note 5, at 15 (noting a difference between *compromise* and *settlement*, but also noting that they "have been used with a variety of meanings and even synonymously").

8. Indemnification

.   .   .

8.3 Legal Action Against the Indemnified Party

(A) *Notice of the Action*

A party that seeks indemnity under § 1.7, 8.1, or 8.2 must promptly give the other party notice of any legal action. But a delay in notice does not relieve an indemnifying party of any liability to an indemnified party, except to the extent that the indemnifying party shows that the delay prejudiced the defense of the action.

(B) *Participating in or Assuming the Defense*

The indemnifying party may participate in the defense at any time. Or it may assume the defense by giving notice to the other party. After assuming the defense, the indemnifying party:

(1) must select an attorney that is satisfactory to the other party;

(2) is not liable to the other party for any later attorney's fees or for any other later expenses that the other party incurs, except for reasonable investigation costs;

(3) must not compromise or settle the action without the other party's consent (but the other party must not unreasonably withhold its consent); and

(4) is not liable for any compromise or settlement made without its consent. [Or omit this item as obvious?]

(C) *Failing to Assume the Defense*

If the indemnifying party fails to assume the defense within 10 days after receiving notice of the action, the indemnifying party is bound by any determination made in the action or by any compromise or settlement made by the other party.

Letting Go of the Myth

The choice is not between precision and plain language. Plain language can be at least as precise — or as appropriately vague — as traditional legal writing. The choice is between perpetuating the vices of four centuries and finally breaking free, between inertia and advancement, between defending the indefensible and opening our minds.

Lawyers continue to write in a style so impenetrable that even other lawyers have trouble understanding it — as the debate over the indemnification clause once again confirms. What would we think of engineers or doctors if they regularly could not understand what another engineer or another doctor had written? Do you suppose that the public's impression of lawyers is in any way influenced by our strange talk and even stranger writing?

I know that, in law, change is hard and progress is slow. But when it comes to legal drafting — contracts, wills and trusts, statutes, ordinances — progress is glacial. Why so? One possible explanation is that legal drafters are blindly overconfident. They believe that because their forms have been around a long time, the forms must be tried and true — a grossly exaggerated notion.[7] Or perhaps the explanation

---

[7] *See* David Mellinkoff, *The Language of the Law* 278–79, 375 (1963) ("[T]he formbooks . . . were decorated with decisions that had never passed on the language or arrangement of the form. . . . [Moreover,] that vast storehouse of judicial definitions known as *Words and Phrases* . . . is an impressive demonstration of lack of precision in the language of the law. And this lack of precision is demonstrated by the very device supposed to give law language its precision — precedent."); Centre for Plain Legal Language, *Law Words: 30 Essays on Legal Words & Phrases* (Mark Duckworth & Arthur Spyrou eds., 1995) (showing that a number of legal terms, like *force majeure* and *right, title, and interest*, are not precise or not required by precedent); Mark Adler, *Tried and Tested: The Myth Behind the Cliché*, Clarity No. 34, at 45 (Jan. 1996) (showing that a typically verbose repair clause in a lease is not required by precedent); Benson Barr, George Hathaway, Nancy Omichinski & Diana Pratt, *Legalese and the Myth of Case Precedent*, 64 Mich. B.J. 1136, 1137 (Oct. 1985) (finding that less than 3% of the words in a real-estate sales contract had significant legal meaning based on precedent).

is that legal drafters recognize that everyone else's drafting is poor, but they can't quite see the same deficiencies in their own work. Now, that's what you'd call a severely limited critical sense. Yet Bryan Garner, our leading authority on legal writing, offers this evidence from years of teaching:

> In my CLE seminars on legal drafting, I routinely ask audience members to answer two questions:
>
> (1) What percentage of the legal drafting that you see is of a genuinely high quality?
> (2) What percentage of legal drafters would claim to produce high-quality drafting?
>
> Although there's some variation within any audience, the consensus is quite predictable: the lawyers say that 5% of the legal drafting they see is of a genuinely high quality, and that 95% of the drafters would claim to produce high-quality documents.
>
> There's a big gap there. It signals that there's still much consciousness-raising needed within the profession — especially on the transactional side.[8]

Garner asserts that, in general, while litigators are very interested in trying to improve their writing, transactional lawyers are not.

In the end, the shame for legal writing is not just that even lawyers have trouble translating it. The shame is that legal writing so often and so unduly needs translating because lawyers don't write in plain language to begin with.

I give the last word on all this to the Law Reform Commission of Victoria (Australia), which in the mid-1980s produced a monumental four-volume study on plain language. Here is what the Commission said about one of its revisory projects:

---

[8] Bryan A. Garner, *President's Letter*, The Scrivener (newsletter of Scribes — Am. Socy. of Writers on Legal Subjects) 1, 3 (Winter 1998).

If some detail has been missed, it could readily be included without affecting the style of the plain English version. It would not be necessary to resort to the convoluted and repetitious style of the original . . . . Any errors in the plain English version are the result of difficulties of translation, particularly difficulties in understanding the original version. They are not inherent in plain English itself. Ideally, of course, plain English should not involve a translation. It should be written from the beginning.[9]

---

[9] Law Reform Commn. of Victoria, *Plain English and the Law* 49 (1987; repr. 1990).

Don't Stop Now:
An Open Letter to the SEC

In January 1997, the Securities and Exchange Commission issued a proposed rule to require plain English in certain parts of prospectuses — the front and back cover pages, the summary, and the risk-factors section. 62 Federal Register 3152 (Jan. 21, 1997). At the same time, the SEC issued the draft text of *A Plain English Handbook: How to Create Clear SEC Disclosure Documents*. I published the letter below in the August 1997 column.

Both the proposed rule and the *Handbook* included many before-and-after examples. In addition, the SEC and several companies had worked together on two pilot programs that produced a number of documents written in plain English. So much for the argument that some matters are too complex for plain English.

In January 1998, the rule was adopted as 17 C.F.R. § 230.421(b), (d). The final version of the *Handbook* is available at http://www.sec.gov/pdf/handbook.pdf.

∽ ∽ ∽

Jonathan G. Katz
Secretary, Securities and Exchange Commission
450 Fifth Street, N.W.
Washington, DC 20549-6009

Dear Mr. Katz:

I write to strongly support the SEC's proposed rule to require plain English in prospectuses (File No. S7-3-97).

First, a word about my background. I have taught legal writing for 13 years at Thomas Cooley Law School. Before that, I was a practicing lawyer. I edit a journal and a monthly column devoted to legal writing, and I've written extensively on plain language. So I'm familiar with these issues.

Now, the SEC's proposed rule and *Plain English Handbook* do an excellent job of setting out the theory and practice of plain English. The rule disposes of the typical criticisms of plain English, and it sets out well-accepted principles for clear writing. The *Handbook* shows in more detail how to apply those principles. Both the rule and the *Handbook* contain many before-and-after examples of how disclosure documents can be improved.

Also, you have rightly taken a flexible approach to plain English. As the *Handbook* says (page 21), "we are presenting guidelines, not hard and fast rules you must always follow." Of course a writer may occasionally have a good reason for using the passive voice. Of course not every sentence has to have fewer than 25 words (especially if it ends with a list). Of course a technical term may be unavoidable at times (although the writer can still explain what it means). But the need for some flexibility does not begin to justify the current state of writing in prospectuses.

I urge the SEC: please, please do not be dissuaded by the lawyers. They always raise the same arguments. And for anyone who has fairly reviewed the plain-English literature, those arguments do not hold water. We have answered them again and again.

First, the argument that plain English is not precise enough for complex material. I have dealt with this argument, and so has the SEC in its proposed rule. In one demonstration project after another — including the SEC's own pilot programs — we have shown that legal documents can be written in much plainer language without any loss of precision. I'll bet that the SEC got hardly any comments that its pilot-program plain-English documents were imprecise or inaccurate. That's proof that it can be done and that traditional documents are full of needless complexity.

If anything, plain English is more precise than traditional legal writing because plain English lays bare the ambiguities and uncertainties that traditional writing — with all its convoluted language and unnecessary detail — tends to hide. In every project that I have worked on, we have found that the original document was not nearly as precise as everyone had thought. So plain English improves not just the style of the document, but the substance as well.

Second, the argument that plain English is impossible because of the need to use technical terms. But true technical terms or terms of art are a tiny part of most legal documents — maybe 2 or 3% of the words. The rest can be written in plain English. And again, even technical terms can usually be explained for consumers.

Third, the argument that plain English is subjective. The truth is that all law is more or less subjective because law depends on language, and language will always involve uncertainty at the margins. What is "reasonable doubt"? What is "good cause"? Does "highway" include the shoulder and the traffic signs? Trying to define everything — as legal documents are inclined to do — is often self-defeating; it complicates the document and still leaves uncertainty.

Beyond that, the history of plain-English requirements shows that they are not too subjective for effective compliance. Ten states now have statutes that require plain English in consumer documents. On the whole, those statutes are pretty consistent with the elements of plain English in the SEC's proposed rule. And by all accounts, those statutes have been successful.

I have a letter from the regulatory officer who reviews contracts for compliance in New Jersey. She writes:

> The New Jersey Plain Language Law has proved to be extremely effective, and the review system is working well. After some initial unease, all segments of the legal

> profession, the legal publishing industry, other large suppliers of contracts, and individual businesses have cooperated fully.... Contrary to fears, no disruptions of business or major problems arose in any industry because of the new consumer-contract standards.

After 14 years in New Jersey, there have been exactly four lawsuits over noncompliance with the plain-language statute. The Minnesota statute has also been in place for 14 years. In Minnesota, there has not been a single lawsuit.

Finally, the argument that compliance should be voluntary. That would be nice, but it probably won't happen. As the proposed rule points out, the SEC has been trying for 30 years to get issuers to improve their prospectuses. Nothing changes. And unless the SEC follows through with its rule, I doubt that anything will change.

I'll end on a personal note. I have been involved in this effort for a long time. I have written that plain language is probably the most important law-reform issue that faces our profession. Even after centuries of criticism, most legal writing remains too long, too dense, and too arcane. It's time to move lawyers off dead center. They owe it to the public to finally stand back, look at the evidence, learn the techniques, and stop copying the old forms. Otherwise, we'll continue to pay the enormous social costs of poor writing in business and government and law.

The SEC is doing the right thing. Don't stop now.

Sincerely,

Joseph Kimble

Joseph Kimble
Professor

The Struggle Against
Suspect Arguments

This column, published in November 2004, responded to two letters to the *Michigan Bar Journal*, as well as a short opinion piece called "The War Against Words."

The gist of the two letters should be clear from the response. In "The War Against Words," the writer began by asserting that the plain-language movement "has degenerated into a verbal witch hunt . . . in which the goal seems to be to . . . attack harmless phrases in any legal writing with the vigor of Moses crushing the golden calf." She then argued that, since skilled readers process hundreds of words a minute, the time it takes to comprehend a few excess words is trivial. She ended with "Plain English, yes. Pale English, no."

∾ ∾ ∾

I'd like to respond not only to Barbara Goldman's complaint about a "War Against Words," but also to the September letter from Cameron Phillips and this month's letter from Thomas Dilley.

Anyone who has followed this column over the last 20 years will know that I have answered these criticisms many times before.[1] This time, I have to do it in an abbreviated way.

---

[1] *See, e.g., Strike Three for Legalese* (May 1990), this book at 3, 9–12; *Plain Words* (Aug. 2001), this book at 163, 163–64.

First, in answer to the Phillips and Dilley letters:

(1) Mr. Dilley refers to those "engaged in the practice, as opposed to the teaching, of law." I practiced. Mr. Phillips mentioned that he was an "English Comp" major. For me, it was English Lit.

(2) Although I've tried to poke fun at a few individual words and phrases in the last four columns, I want to remind readers that preferring familiar words (usually the shorter ones) is only one element of plain language — one among dozens that I listed in the October 2002 column.[2] Plain language, rightly understood, involves all the techniques for clear communication: planning a document, designing it, organizing it, constructing sentences, choosing words, and testing mass documents on typical readers. Check the October 2002 column, and I think you'll see that the guidelines are varied and flexible.

(3) For each of the words and phrases in these last four columns, I cited at least five legal-writing experts who recommend against using them. The Phillips and Dilley letters cite no contrary authorities. In fact, they cite no authority at all for any of their arguments. Would they go into court without any authority?

(4) Mr. Dilley refers to "the implicit suggestion that lawyers generally are guilty of willful obfuscation in oral and written presentations." I have never said or implied that. I have said that our linguistic plight is caused by centuries of poor models, bad habits, and inadequate training — not to mention the kind of resistance to change that these two letters reflect.

(5) Mr. Phillips emphasizes the need for "certainty" in legal writing. Likewise, Mr. Dilley refers to the need for "subtle, precise" language. This is the myth of precision — the notion that traditional legal writing is more precise than plain language. That myth has been debunked by our two great scholars of legal language, David Mellinkoff and Bryan

---

[2] *The Elements of Plain Language*, this book at 69.

Garner.[3] If anything, the opposite is true because plain language uncovers the ambiguities and errors that lie hidden under the dense, murky surface of traditional style.[4] I could cite many examples from the major projects to restyle the Federal Rules of Criminal Procedure (completed in 2001) and the Federal Rules of Civil Procedure (published for comment in February 2005).[5]

(6) Mr. Phillips charges that I seem to advocate "the writing style of a fourth grader." Mr. Dilley makes a similar comment about what can be understood by "your average third grader." This is the most stubborn and most profoundly distorted of all the criticisms of plain language. Plain language is, at bottom, about writing clearly and effectively for your intended reader. Have you ever heard anyone object that a piece of legal writing is too clear? Moreover, a clear, plain style — far from being unsophisticated — only *looks* easy; it takes skill and hard work. And it has a long literary tradition. (See the quote from Jacques Barzun below, pages 57–58.)

(7) Mr. Dilley asserts that "the great protectors of the integrity of the English Language . . . may be found in only three spheres: the ministry, the Senate, and the legal profession." I'm sorry to say that, by nearly all accounts, the history of legal writing is anything but glorious. It has been criticized, even ridiculed, by everyone from Jonathan Swift to Thomas Jefferson to Fred Rodell. David Mellinkoff, in his classic study, describes legal writing as having four main characteristics: it's wordy, unclear, pompous, and dull.[6] Bryan Garner says that lawyers "have a history of wretched

---

[3] David Mellinkoff, *The Language of the Law* 290–398 (1963); Bryan A. Garner, *A Dictionary of Modern Legal Usage* 580 (2d ed. 1995).

[4] See *The Great Myth That Plain Language Is Not Precise*, this book at 37.

[5] See *How to Mangle Court Rules and Jury Instructions*, this book at 105, 121–22 & n. 44.

[6] Mellinkoff, *supra* note 3, at 24.

writing, a history that reinforces itself every time we open the law books."[7] John Lindsey adds that law books are "the largest body of poorly written literature ever created by the human race."[8]

Now a response to Ms. Goldman's comments about the dubious value of eliminating excess words:

(1) Reading and readability are complex and controversial. The most commonly used readability formulas, to the extent they have any validity, depend on how long the sentences are and on how long or familiar the words are.

(2) Of course, a few extra words here and there will not affect a piece of writing. But the cumulative effect of a lot of extra words surely will. Consider the logical extension of Ms. Goldman's argument. Does she mean to say that wordiness and inflated diction don't matter enough to be worth fixing? Every writing book and style guide on the planet says otherwise. Here are a few, by authors you may recognize:

> Writing is devilish; the general sin is wordiness. We put down the first thought that comes, we miss the best order, and we then need lengths of *is*'s, *of*s, *by*s, and *which*s — words virtually meaningless in themselves — to wire our meaningful words together again. . . . If you can rephrase to save even one word, your sentence will be clearer.[9]

> [T]he secret of good writing is to strip every sentence to its cleanest components. Every word that serves no function, every long word that could be a short word, every adverb that carries the same meaning that's already in the verb, every passive construction that leaves the reader unsure of who is doing what — these are the thousand and one adulterants that weaken the strength of a sentence.[10]

---

[7] Bryan A. Garner, *The Elements of Legal Style* 2 (2d ed. 2002).

[8] John M. Lindsey, *The Legal Writing Malady: Causes and Cures*, 204 N.Y. L.J. 2 (Dec. 12, 1990).

[9] Sheridan Baker, *The Practical Stylist* 111, 112 (8th ed. 1998).

[10] William Zinsser, *On Writing Well* 7–8 (6th rev. ed. 2001).

Ruthlessly cut unnecessary words. When you use fewer words to express an idea, you enhance your writing's speed, clarity, and impact. Conversely, when you use more words than necessary, you make the writing slower, less clear, and less emphatic. That's why you should take it seriously whenever someone points out a shorter way of saying something. You save here and there, and soon your savings will grow into something quite valuable.[11]

Omit needless words. Vigorous writing is concise. A sentence should contain no unnecessary words . . . for the same reason that a drawing should have no unnecessary lines and a machine no unnecessary parts. . . . **Avoid fancy words.** Avoid the elaborate, the pretentious, the coy, and the cute. Do not be tempted by a twenty-dollar word when there is a ten-center handy, ready and able.[12]

(3) Apart from sheer word count, a phrase like *prior to* often leads to clumsy, indirect constructions. It's symptomatic, if you will. Example: "This will be the last recorded message you hear prior to your call being answered." Or: "Prior to the argument by the attorneys on the objection, the court excused the jury." Imagine if Frost had written "And miles to go prior to my sleeping."

(4) In short, there is always the matter of tone, of the impression your writing makes. Consider this from Jacques Barzun:

> [T]he best tone is the tone called plain, unaffected, unadorned. . . . It is the most difficult of all tones, and also the most adaptable. When you can write plain, you can trust yourself in special effects. The plain tone is that of Lincoln always, that of Thoreau, Emerson, William James, Mark Twain, "Mr. Dooley," Fitzgerald, and Hemingway at their best. It is the tone Whitman urged on his contemporaries: "The art of art, the glory of expression

---

[11] Bryan A. Garner, *The Winning Brief* 212 (2d ed. 2004).

[12] William Strunk, Jr. & E.B. White, *The Elements of Style* 23, 76–77 (4th ed. 2000).

...is simplicity. Nothing is better than simplicity ...
nothing can make up for excess or for the lack of
definiteness."[13]

(5) As far as testing goes, there is a great deal of
empirical evidence that plain language, taken as a whole,
improves readers' comprehension of legal documents.[14] And
there is evidence that readers strongly prefer plain language
in legal and official documents.[15] In fact, some of the first
testing of legal documents was reported in this column, in
October 1987 and May 1990. When judges and lawyers in
four states, including Michigan, were asked to choose
between the A and B versions of different passages from
legal documents, they preferred the plain-language versions
by overwhelming margins in all four states.[16]

(6) Ms. Goldman ends with "Pale English, no." This is
a first cousin to the grade-school argument discussed earlier.
Does she really think that provisos and *prior to* and *in terms
of* breathe life into prose? More likely to deaden it, I'd say.

In the August and September 2001 columns, called
"Plain Words," I offered lists of words and phrases that
writers might consider replacing. I included several
qualifications and cautions, yet still made this prediction: "I
will be accused of promoting baby talk, of constricting and
dumbing down the language, of denying writers their
expressive voice, and of corrupting legal discourse."[17]

No wild predictions this time. I'll just invite all writers
to consider the evidence, consult the books on writing, keep
reading the column, and make your own choices.

---

[13] Jacques Barzun, *Simple and Direct: A Rhetoric for Writers* 90 (rev. ed.
1985).

[14] *See Answering the Critics of Plain Language*, 5 Scribes J. Legal Writing
51, 62–65 (1994–1995).

[15] *See Writing for Dollars, Writing to Please*, 6 Scribes J. Legal Writing 1,
19–31 (1996–1997).

[16] *Strike Three for Legalese*, this book at 13.

[17] *Plain Words*, this book at 163.

You Be the Judge

All too often, the debate over plain legal language is abstract and theoretical. We form impressions about how legal writing should "sound" or what kind of style will be most "effective" or what courts and clients "prefer." And we misjudge what it means to write in plain language. So let's get concrete.

For more than two years, the federal Advisory Committee on Civil Rules engaged in a huge project to "restyle" the Federal Rules of Civil Procedure. The project produced more than 600 documents scrutinizing every sentence, word, and comma, and the restyled rules were published for comment in February 2005.

On the next three pages are some short before-and-after examples. You be the judge. Which one is clearer? Which one would you prefer to read? Which one would you prefer to have written? Which one reflects better on the legal profession?

There is already a body of strong empirical evidence that "plain language saves money and pleases readers: it is much more likely to be read and understood and heeded — in much less time."[1] Now I invite you to consider the evidence of your own senses.

---

[1] *Writing for Dollars, Writing to Please*, 6 Scribes J. Legal Writing 1, 37 (1996–1997) (summarizing the results of dozens of studies).

Current Rule 8(e)(2)

When two or more statements are made in the alternative and one of them if made independently would be sufficient, the pleading is not made insufficient by the insufficiency of one or more of the alternative statements.

Restyled Rule

If a party makes alternative statements, the pleading is sufficient if any one of them is sufficient.

Current Rule 30(g)

(1) If the party giving the notice of the taking of a deposition fails to attend and proceed therewith and another party attends in person or by attorney pursuant to the notice, the court may order the party giving the notice to pay to such other party the reasonable expenses incurred by that party and that party's attorney in attending, including reasonable attorney's fees.

(2) If the party giving the notice of the taking of a deposition of a witness fails to serve a subpoena upon the witness and the witness because of such failure does not attend, and if another party attends in person or by attorney because that party expects the deposition of that witness to be taken, the court may order the party giving the notice to pay to such other party the reasonable expenses incurred by that party and that party's attorney in attending, including reasonable attorney's fees.

Restyled Rule

A party who, expecting a deposition to be taken, attends in person or by an attorney may recover reasonable expenses for attending, including attorney's fees, if the noticing party failed to:

(1) attend and proceed with the deposition; or

(2) serve a subpoena on a nonparty deponent, who consequently did not attend.

Current Rule 50(b)

In ruling on a renewed motion, the court may:

(1) if a verdict was returned:

    (A) allow the judgment to stand,

    (B) order a new trial, or

    (C) direct entry of judgment as a matter of law; or

(2) if no verdict was returned:

    (A) order a new trial, or

    (B) direct entry of judgment as a matter of law.

Restyled Rule

In ruling on the renewed motion, the court may:

(1) allow judgment on the verdict, if the jury returned a verdict;

(2) order a new trial; or

(3) direct the entry of judgment as a matter of law.

Current Rule 56(e)

Supporting and opposing affidavits shall be made on personal knowledge, shall set forth such facts as would be admissible in evidence, and shall show affirmatively that the affiant is competent to testify to the matters stated therein. Sworn or certified copies of all papers or parts thereof referred to in an affidavit shall be attached thereto or served therewith.

Restyled Rule

A supporting or opposing affidavit must be made on personal knowledge, set out facts that would be admissible in evidence, and show that the affiant is competent to testify on the matters stated. If a paper or part of a paper is referred to in an affidavit, a sworn or certified copy must be attached to or served with the affidavit.

Current Rule 69(a)

The procedure on execution, in proceedings supplementary to and in aid of a judgment, and in proceedings on and in aid of execution shall be in accordance with the practice and procedure of the state in which the district court is held, existing at the time the remedy is sought, except that any statute of the United States governs to the extent that it is applicable.

Restyled Rule

The procedure on execution — and in proceedings supplementary to and in aid of judgment or execution — must follow the procedure of the state where the court is located, but a federal statute governs to the extent it applies.

Current Rule 71A(k)

The practice as herein prescribed governs in actions involving the exercise of the power of eminent domain under the law of a state, provided that if the state law makes provision for trial of any issue by jury, or for trial of the issue of compensation by jury or commission or both, that provision shall be followed.

Restyled Rule

This rule governs an action involving eminent domain under state law. But if state law provides for trying an issue by jury — or for trying the issue of compensation by jury or commission or both — that law governs.

You Be the Judge (Again)

In the previous essay, I suggested that instead of debating about plain language in the abstract, we might better look at empirical evidence and concrete examples. Otherwise, we may never get past the myths, misconceptions, and mischaracterizations that continue to cloud the debate and discourage reform.

The empirical evidence, once again, is all on the side of plain language. As for concrete examples, I invited you in that last essay to consider some before-and-after examples from the momentous two-year project to "restyle" the Federal Rules of Civil Procedure. Those examples mainly illustrated differences at the sentence level. Now I offer one longer example that illustrates differences in design (formatting) and organization.

As you look over the restyled rule, please ask yourself a few questions. Would you describe it as using grade-school prose? Does it dumb down the language? Does it change the meaning? Is it less precise than the current rule? Does it subvert any technical terms?

If you answered no to these questions, then you have adjudged the common criticisms of plain language to be unfounded.

Current Rule 14(a)

(a) **When Defendant May Bring in Third Party.** At any time after commencement of the action a defending party, as a third-party plaintiff, may cause a summons and complaint to be served upon a person not a party to the action who is or may be liable to the third-party plaintiff for all or part of the plaintiff's claim against the third-party plaintiff. The third-party plaintiff need not obtain leave to make the service if the third-party plaintiff files the third-party complaint not later than 10 days after serving the original answer. Otherwise the third-party plaintiff must obtain leave on motion upon notice to all parties to the action. The person served with the summons and third-party complaint, hereinafter called the third-party defendant, shall make any defenses to the third-party plaintiff's claim as provided in Rule 12 and any counterclaims against the third-party plaintiff and cross-claims against other third-party defendants as provided in Rule 13. The third-party defendant may assert against the plaintiff any defenses which the third-party plaintiff has to the plaintiff's claim. The third-party defendant may also assert any claim against the plaintiff arising out of the transaction or occurrence that is the subject matter of the plaintiff's claim against the third-party plaintiff. The plaintiff may assert any claim against the third-party defendant arising out of the transaction or occurrence that is the subject matter of the plaintiff's claim against the third-party plaintiff, and the third-party defendant thereupon shall assert any defenses as provided in Rule 12 and any counterclaims and cross-claims as provided in Rule 13. Any party may move to strike the third-party claim, or for its severance or separate trial. A third-party defendant may proceed under this rule against any person not a party to the action who is or may be liable to the third-party defendant for all or part of the claim made in the action against the third-party defendant. The third-party complaint, if within the admiralty and maritime jurisdiction, may be in rem against a vessel, cargo, or other property subject to admiralty or maritime process in rem, in which case references in this rule to the summons include the warrant of arrest, and references to the third-party plaintiff or defendant include, where appropriate, a person who asserts a right under Supplemental Rule C(6)(b)(i) in the property arrested.

Restyled Rule 14(a)

(a) When a Defending Party May Bring in a Third Party.

(1) *Timing of the Summons and Complaint.* A defending party may, as third-party plaintiff, serve a summons and complaint on a nonparty who is or may be liable to it for all or part of the claim against it. But the third-party plaintiff must, by motion, obtain the court's leave if it files the third-party complaint more than 10 days after serving its original answer.

(2) *Third-Party Defendant's Claims and Defenses.* The person served with the summons and third-party complaint — the "third-party defendant":

  (A) must assert any defense against the third-party plaintiff's claim under Rule 12;

  (B) must assert any counterclaim against the third-party plaintiff under Rule 13(a), and may assert any counterclaim against the third-party plaintiff under Rule 13(b) or any crossclaim against another third-party defendant under Rule 13(g);

  (C) may assert against the plaintiff any defense that the third-party plaintiff has to the plaintiff's claim; and

  (D) may also assert against the plaintiff any claim arising out of the transaction or occurrence that is the subject matter of the plaintiff's claim against the third-party plaintiff.

(3) *Plaintiff's Claims Against a Third-Party Defendant.* The plaintiff may assert against the third-party defendant any claim arising out of the transaction or occurrence that is the subject matter of the plaintiff's claim against the third-party plaintiff. The third-party defendant must then assert any defense under Rule 12 and any counterclaim under Rule 13(a), and may assert any counterclaim under Rule 13(b) or any crossclaim under Rule 13(g).

(4) *Motion to Strike, Sever, or Try Separately.* Any party may move to strike the third-party claim, to sever it, or to try it separately.

(5) ***Third-Party Defendant's Claim Against a Nonparty.*** A third-party defendant may proceed under this rule against a nonparty who is or may be liable to the third-party defendant for all or part of any claim against it.

(6) ***Third-Party Complaint in Rem.*** If it is within the admiralty or maritime jurisdiction, a third-party complaint may be in rem. In that event, a reference in this rule to the "summons" includes the warrant of arrest, and a reference to the defendant or third-party plaintiff includes, when appropriate, a person who asserts a right under Supplemental Rule C(6)(b)(i) in the property arrested.

PART TWO

Some Advice and Some More Examples

The Elements of Plain Language

I originally published these guidelines in 1992, in the *Thomas M. Cooley Law Review*.[1] I then tinkered with them ten years later, for the October 2002 column.

∾ ∾ ∾

A. In General

1. As the starting point and at every point, design and write the document in a way that best serves the reader. Your main goal is to convey your ideas with the greatest possible clarity.
2. Resist the urge to sound formal. Relax and be natural (but not too informal). Try for the same unaffected tone you would use if you were speaking to the reader in person.
3. Omit unnecessary detail. Boil down the information to what your reader needs to know.
4. Use examples as needed to help explain the text.
5. Whenever possible, test consumer documents on a small group of typical users — and improve the documents as need be.

---

[1] *Plain English: A Charter for Clear Writing*, 9 Thomas M. Cooley L. Rev. 1, 11–14 (1992).

B. Design

1. Make a table of contents for long documents.
2. Use at least 10- to 12-point type for text, and a readable serif typeface.
3. Try to use between 50 and 70 characters a line.
4. Use ample white space in margins, between sections, and around headings and other special items.
5. Use highlighting techniques such as boldface, italics, and bullet dots. But don't overdo them, and be consistent throughout the document.
6. Avoid using all-capital letters. And avoid overusing initial capitals for common nouns (*this agreement, trust, common stock*).
7. Use diagrams, tables, and charts as needed to help explain the text.

C. Organization

1. Use short sections, or subdivide longer ones.
2. Put related material together.
3. Order the parts in a logical sequence. Normally, put the more important before the less important, the general before the specific, and the ordinary before the extraordinary.
4. Use informative headings for the main divisions and subdivisions. In consumer documents, try putting the main headings in the form of a question.
5. Minimize cross-references.
6. Minimize definitions. If you have more than a few, put them in a separate glossary at the end of the document.

(The next four items apply to analytical documents, such as briefs and memos, and to most informational documents.)

7. Try to begin the document and the main divisions with one or two paragraphs that introduce and summarize what follows, including your answer.
8. Use a topic sentence to summarize the main idea of each paragraph or of a series of paragraphs on the same topic.
9. Make sure that each paragraph develops the main idea through a logical sequence of sentences.
10. Use transitions to link the ideas and introduce new ideas.

D. Sentences

1. Prefer short and medium-length sentences. As a guideline, keep the average length to about 20 words.
2. Don't pile up a series of conditions or qualifiers before the main clause.
3. In most sentences, put the subject near the beginning; keep it short and concrete; make it something the reader already knows about; and make it the agent of the action in the verb.
4. Put the central action in strong verbs, not in abstract nouns. ("If the seller delivers the goods late, the buyer may cancel the contract." Not: "Late delivery of the goods may result in cancellation of the contract.")
5. Keep the subject near the verb, and the verb near the object (or complement). Avoid intrusive phrases and clauses.
6. Put the strongest point, your most important information, at the end — where the emphasis falls.
7. Prefer the active voice. Use the passive voice if the agent is unknown or unimportant. Or use it if, for continuity, you want to focus attention on the object of the action instead of the agent. ("No more legalese. It has been ridiculed long enough.")

8. Connect modifying words to what they modify. Be especially careful with a series: make clear whether the modifier applies to one or more than one item. (Examples of ambiguity: "educational institutions or corporations"; "a felony or misdemeanor involving dishonesty.")
9. Use parallel structure for parallel ideas. Consider using a list if the items are at all complicated, as when you have multiple conditions, consequences, or rules. And put the list at the end of the sentence.

E. Words

1. Prefer familiar words — usually the shorter ones — that are simple and direct and human.
2. Avoid unnecessary jargon: stuffy old formalisms (*Now comes*; *In witness whereof*); here-, there-, and where-words (*hereby*, *therein*, *wherefore*); needless Latin (*arguendo, inter alia, sub silentio*); and all the rest (*and/or, provided that, pursuant to, the instant case*).
3. Avoid doublets and triplets (*any and all*; *give, devise, and bequeath*).
4. In consumer documents, explain technical terms that you cannot avoid using.
5. Omit unnecessary words.
6. Replace wordy phrases. Take special aim at multiword prepositions (*prior to, with regard to, in connection with*). And treat the word *of* as a good indicator of possible flab (*the duty of the landlord, an order of the court*).
7. Banish *shall*; use *must* instead.
8. In consumer documents, consider making the consumer "you."
9. Avoid multiple negatives.
10. Be consistent; use the same term for the same thing, especially in drafting.

First Things First:
The Lost Art of Summarizing

If you value clarity, if you insist on lighting the way for your reader, then you'll provide good summaries where they belong in just about every piece of legal writing: up front. You should always have one at the beginning or near the beginning, and if you're dealing with multiple issues, you should have one at the beginning of each issue. Call them what you will — summaries, overviews, brief answers, thesis statements, synopses — they are central to clear writing:

> A vast amount of empirical research has studied the effects of overviews on learning from written prose. The research support for this principle is broad and consistent. ... [T]he support is sufficiently broad to establish the general value of overviews for understanding written text in any environment and for any audience.[1]

All legal writing should be front-loaded. It should start with a capsule version of the analysis. It should practice the art of summarizing.

Summaries in Judicial Opinions —
The Opening Paragraphs

An often-quoted article on writing opinions gives this advice:

> The importance of the first paragraph cannot be over-emphasized. ... The readability of an opinion is nearly

---

[1] Daniel B. Felker, Frances Pickering, Veda R. Charrow, V. Melissa Holland & Janice C. Redish, *Guidelines for Document Designers* 16 (1981).

always improved if the opening paragraph (occasionally it takes two) answers three questions. First, what kind of case is this: Divorce, foreclosure, workmen's compensation, and so on? Second, what roles, plaintiff or defendant, did the appellant and the appellee have in the trial court? Third, what was the trial court's decision? A fourth question, What are the issues on appeal?, should also be answered unless the contentions are too numerous to be easily summarized.[2]

The advice is incomplete in two respects. It doesn't make clear that the court should set out the deep issue or issues, not just the superficial issues. And just as important, the advice doesn't say that the court should summarize its answers to the deep issues.

The term "deep issue" was coined by Bryan Garner, who explains that "the surface issue does not disclose the decisional premises; the deep issue makes them explicit. It yields up what Justice Holmes once called the 'implements of decision.'"[3] Garner identifies 12 categories of judicial openers along a continuum from "no issue" to "surface issue" to "deep issue." I can hardly add to his exposition, except to say that there will usually be degrees or levels of deepness to choose from and that briefs and memos may require slightly different choices than opinions will. I'll explain these two points more fully in the next two sections.

Meanwhile, let's remind ourselves what clarity — maximal clarity — demands of a judicial opener: (1) the crucial facts; (2) the deep issue, stated explicitly or implicitly in terms of the pertinent legal rule or requirement; and (3) the answer, which may involve simply applying the pertinent

[2] George Rose Smith, *A Primer of Opinion Writing for Four New Judges*, 21 Ark. L. Rev. 197, 204 (1967); *see also* Ruggero J. Aldisert, *Opinion Writing* 72–77 (1990) (citing Smith with approval but also recommending a conclusion in the first paragraph).

[3] Bryan A. Garner, *The Deep Issue: A New Approach to Framing Legal Questions*, 5 Scribes J. Legal Writing 1, 4 (1994–1995) (citation omitted).

rule, or choosing between two possible rules, or sometimes applying an even deeper rule that I'll call the dispositive rule. Note that the answer goes beyond a mere yes or no; it includes the reasoning. All this may seem complicated, but you'll have no trouble identifying these parts in a good opener.

The only trouble is in finding good ones. (Are you surprised?) For instance, I looked at Volume 462 of the *Michigan Reports*, the most recent bound volume as I was writing. The first four opinions are per curiam opinions, with first paragraphs like this (it's one of the better ones):

> The defendant was convicted of delivering between 50 and 225 grams of cocaine, which presumptively requires a prison term of ten to twenty years. The trial court concluded that there were substantial and compelling reasons for departing from the statutory mandate, however, and imposed a prison term of five to twenty years. We agree with the dissenting judge in the Court of Appeals that the trial court considered an inappropriate factor in concluding that a departure was warranted. We thus reverse and remand to the trial court for resentencing.[4]

But the deep issue there was whether a defendant's expression of remorse is an objective and verifiable factor. It could have been included so easily: "We agree with the dissenting judge in the Court of Appeals that the trial court inappropriately considered a factor that was not objective and verifiable — defendant's expression of remorse." That one sentence identifies the pertinent rule and applies it to the crucial facts.

After the four per curiams comes an authored opinion with these first two paragraphs:

> The question in these consolidated appeals is whether the state of Michigan was barred by [a statute] from indicting defendants for conspiracy to possess with intent to deliver more than 650 grams of a mixture containing

---

[4] *People v. Daniel*, 609 N.W.2d 557, 557–58 (Mich. 2000).

cocaine when they had previously been convicted in federal court in Florida of conspiracy to possess with intent to distribute more than five kilograms of cocaine.

I would hold that the state prosecution was not barred by [the statute] because conspiracy charges are not a violation of "this article" (article 7 of the Public Health Code) for purposes of the statute. The statute does not apply because the conspiracy charges arose under chapter 24 of the Penal Code, not under article 7 of the Public Health Code. Therefore, I would reverse the judgments of the trial court and Court of Appeals and reinstate defendants' convictions.[5]

That just about gets it. That gets to the deep issue (although, unfortunately, (1) you have to read a footnote to find the statutory rule against double convictions for violating "this article," and (2) the initial paragraph is a 62-word sentence in reverse chronological order). Notice the two uses of *because* in the second paragraph. That's a good sign. *Because* is the word that signals an answer, the word that almost forces the writer to explain.

I spent a long day reading all the opinions in Volume 462. By my reckoning, only 9 of the 27 opinions set out the deep issue, coupled with an answer, in the opening paragraphs. Here's another one that does; the court is choosing from possible rules:

In this premises liability case the plaintiff, Violet Moeller, was injured when she tripped over a concrete tire stop in defendant church's parking lot. Plaintiff was visiting the church to attend bible study. Plaintiff sued the church, alleging that the defendant negligently placed the tire stops and failed to provide adequate lighting in the parking lot.

At trial, the jury was instructed on the obligations property owners owe to licensees. The jury returned a verdict in favor of the church. The Court of Appeals

---

[5] *People v. Hermiz*, 611 N.W.2d 783, 784 (Mich. 2000) (citations omitted).

reversed and remanded the case for a new trial after determining that the trial court erred by instructing the jury on the obligations owed to licensees rather than "public invitees" as defined in 2 Restatement Torts, 2d, § 332, p. 176.

We granted leave in this case to determine the proper standard of care owed to individuals on church property for noncommercial purposes. We hold that the trial court correctly instructed the jury that such individuals are licensees and not invitees. Accordingly, we reverse the Court of Appeals decision and reinstate the trial court judgment in favor of the church.[6]

This could have been shorter, though, especially since the next section of the opinion is called "Factual and Procedural Background." A revised version:

In this premises-liability case, the plaintiff, Violet Moeller, was injured when she tripped over a concrete tire stop in defendant church's parking lot. She was visiting the church to attend Bible study. The Court of Appeals determined that Moeller was not a licensee but rather a "public invitee" as defined in 2 Restatement Torts, 2d, § 332, p. 176. We disagree. We hold that to become an invitee, a person must show that the premises were held open for a commercial purpose. We reject the Restatement's definition of "public invitee."

Finally, from the same volume, here's another incomplete opener:

We consider in this case the trial court's decision to suppress defendant's voluntary confession on the ground that defendant did not "knowingly and intelligently" waive his *Miranda* rights. We conclude that the trial court applied an erroneous legal standard in assessing the validity of defendant's *Miranda* waiver. Moreover, we

---

[6] *Stitt v. Holland Abundant Life Fellowship*, 614 N.W.2d 88, 90 (Mich. 2000) (citations omitted).

conclude that the waiver was valid. Therefore, we reverse the trial court's decision suppressing defendant's confession.[7]

This misses the crucial facts and the dispositive legal rule. A revised version:

> Defendant waived his *Miranda* rights and confessed to murder. According to a psychiatric expert, he was delusional and believed that God would set him free if he confessed. The trial court concluded that his waiver was not "knowing and intelligent" [the pertinent rule]. But the court erred in focusing on why he confessed. The proper test for waiver is whether defendant understands the *Miranda* rights [the dispositive rule], not whether he understands the consequences of waiving them.

Looking Deeper Into One Opinion

Several years ago, to test styles of opinion-writing, I rewrote a fairly routine opinion of the Michigan Court of Appeals. I labeled one version O and the other version Y, and sent them out randomly to several hundred Michigan lawyers. I asked the lawyers which opinion they preferred and why. (For the "why," I included a list of possible reasons.) Result: 61% of 251 lawyers preferred the revised version.[8]

Now, this result was certainly not produced by any one change or technique. Still, the difference between the two opinions' first paragraphs, where the writer should get down to the nitty-gritty, is striking:

---

[7] *People v. Daoud*, 614 N.W.2d 152, 153–54 (Mich. 2000) (citation omitted).

[8] *The Straight Skinny on Better Judicial Opinions*, this book at 15, 19.

Original:

Plaintiff Robert Wills filed a declaratory judgment action against defendant State Farm Insurance Company to determine whether defendant has a duty to pay benefits under the uninsured motorist provisions found in plaintiff's policy with defendant. Pursuant to the parties' stipulated statement of facts, the trial court granted summary disposition in plaintiff's favor upon finding coverage where gunshots fired from an unidentified automobile passing plaintiff's vehicle caused plaintiff to drive off the road and suffer injuries. Defendant appeals as of right. We reverse and remand.[9]

Revised:

Summary

Robert Wills was injured when someone drove by him and fired shots toward his car, causing him to swerve into a tree. He filed a declaratory-judgment action to determine whether State Farm had to pay him uninsured-motorist benefits. The issue is whether there was a "substantial physical nexus" between the unidentified car and Wills's car. The trial court answered yes and granted a summary disposition for Wills. We disagree and reverse. We do not find a substantial physical nexus between the two cars, because the bullets were not projected by the unidentified car itself.

Why does the original fall short? It doesn't get to the deep issue. And it doesn't get to the answer, which in this case involves a deeper, dispositive rule — namely, that "substantial physical nexus" requires contact with something that the phantom car itself projected.

Let me explain what I mean by levels of deepness. All legal analysis is based, explicitly or implicitly, on the deductive reasoning that we recognize as a syllogism. Often, the minor premise of the syllogism involves reasoning by

---

[9] *Wills v. State Farm Ins. Co.*, 564 N.W.2d 488, 489 (Mich. App. 1997).

analogy. In the case I tested, there are four syllogisms; the minor premise of each one depends for its validity on the deeper syllogism that follows it. In the figures below, the a, b, and c stand for major premise (rule), minor premise (related facts), and conclusion. The sentences are not smooth, but I believe that the forms are correct.

1. a. A policyholder must show injury arising from the use of an uninsured motor vehicle to recover under the policy.

   b. The policyholder, Wills, cannot show bodily injury arising from the use of an uninsured motor vehicle.

   c. Therefore, the policyholder cannot recover under the policy.

2. a. Under the policy, a vehicle that has an unknown driver and that "strikes" the insured's vehicle is an uninsured motor vehicle.

   b. The other vehicle had an unknown driver, but it didn't strike the insured's vehicle.

   c. Therefore, the other vehicle was not an uninsured motor vehicle.

3. a. According to previous decisions involving indirect physical contact, a "substantial physical nexus" between the unidentified car and the object it casts off or projects is required for "striking" the insured's vehicle.

   b. There was no substantial physical nexus between the unidentified car and the object it projected.

   c. Therefore, the unidentified car did not strike the insured's vehicle.

4. a. The object must be projected by the unidentified
        car itself to meet the requirement of a
        "substantial physical nexus."

    b. The bullets were not projected by the
        unidentified car itself.

        [Analogy: This case is like another one in which
        someone in the unidentified car shot the
        policyholder while he stood beside his car. This
        case is distinguishable from cases in which the
        unidentified car threw a rock or dropped a piece
        of metal on the road.]

    c. Therefore, the requirement of "substantial
        physical nexus" is not met.

Now you see what's wrong with the original first
paragraph. Although it does state the crucial facts, it barely
gets to the first level of reasoning, the first syllogism; it just
concludes, baldly and superficially, that plaintiff has no
uninsured-motorist coverage. The revised version, on the
other hand, gets down to the last syllogism. It gets down to
the *ratio decidendi*, the dispositive rule.

Summaries in Briefs and Memos

Good summaries in briefs and memos will contain the same
three elements that opinions do: the crucial facts, the deep
issue, and the answer. The differences are mainly structural:
in briefs and memos, the issue is stated explicitly and the
answer follows in a separate part. This may, in turn, present
a choice of how deep to go into the issue.

Let me illustrate with that uninsured-motorist case,
Wills. It's mundane, but typically mundane, and thus a good
example.

Suppose you were stating the issue in the insurance
company's brief. (Incidentally, I'll follow Garner's sensible

advice to not cram everything into a single sentence.[10]) You might start the issue with these facts: "Robert Wills was injured when somebody drove by him and fired shots toward his car, causing him to swerve into a tree. Only the bullets — and nothing from the unidentified car itself — struck Wills's car." Then, as you round out the issue, you have a choice about how deep to go in the sentences that follow those first two. Here are the possibilities, from surface issues to increasingly deeper issues:

- Can Wills recover uninsured-motorist benefits?
- Can Wills show that his injury arose from "the use of an uninsured motor vehicle" as defined in his policy?
- To recover uninsured-motorist benefits under his policy, Wills must show that the unidentified car "struck" his car. Can Wills make that showing?
- To recover uninsured-motorist benefits under his policy, Wills must show that the unidentified car "struck" his car. And according to cases involving indirect "striking," there must be a "substantial physical nexus" between the cars. Can Wills show a substantial physical nexus?
- To recover uninsured-motorist benefits under his policy, Wills must show that the unidentified car "struck" his car. And according to cases involving indirect "striking," there must be a "substantial physical nexus" between the cars created by something that is projected by the unidentified car itself. Can Wills show that the unidentified car itself projected the bullets that hit his car?

You can see that it's increasingly difficult to frame the issue concisely as you go deeper into the levels of analysis. I would probably settle for the third bullet dot. Oddly

---

[10] Garner, *supra* note 3, at 1.

enough, the third formulation seems more persuasive than the fourth, with its vague — and unhelpful — concept of "substantial physical nexus." The third one is more persuasive because the facts (in the first two sentences of the issue) suggest no "striking."

After so stating the issue, you could answer as follows in the Summary of Argument part of your brief:

> Wills's policy with State Farm provides coverage for bodily injury "arising from the use of an uninsured motor vehicle." The policy defines an uninsured motor vehicle as one that has an unknown driver and that "strikes" the insured's vehicle.
>
> In this case, the unidentified car did not strike Wills's car, even indirectly. In other cases involving indirect contact, the Court of Appeals has ruled that the striking object must be cast off or projected from the unidentified car itself; only then is there a "substantial physical nexus" between the two cars. And here the bullets that hit Wills's car were not projected by the unidentified car itself, but by a gun.

Later, of course, would come the Argument section, with a point heading and another summary after the point heading. (Some writing texts call this second summary a thesis statement.) Inevitably, the second summary will require some repetition, but an adroit writer can minimize it. Thus:

> **Plaintiff Wills cannot show that the unidentified car "struck" his car.**
>
> Wills cannot show that the unidentified car "struck" his car, as his policy requires him to do, because he cannot show that the unidentified car *itself* fired the bullets. It's not enough that the bullets came from a gun fired by someone riding in the car.
>
> Here is the policy language at issue . . . .

Now, let's briefly go back. How would you frame the issue for the plaintiff, who of course lost? I suspect that he was trying to distinguish an earlier case in which the policyholder was hit by bullets shot from a moving car as he stood outside his car; the bullets hit him, not his car.[11] So plaintiff Wills might frame his issue like this:

> Robert Wills was injured when somebody drove by him and fired shots that hit his car, causing him to swerve into a tree. The shots from the unidentified car actually hit his car as they were both moving. To recover uninsured-motorist benefits under his policy, Wills must show that the unidentified car "struck" his car. Can Wills make that showing?

Finally, how might you state the issue in an office memo — that is, when you are in objective, not persuasive, mode? In the *Wills* case, the differences are not as substantial as they would be in a more complicated case, with messier, conflicting facts and more arguable rules and policies. So this will sound familiar:

> Robert Wills was injured when somebody drove by him and fired shots that hit his car, causing him to swerve into a tree. To recover uninsured-motorist benefits under his policy, Wills must show that the unidentified car "struck" his car. Can Wills make that showing?

A Brief Answer, which should follow directly, will complete the summary and send the reader down a marked path toward a clear destination. I'll spare you this last example, though. You have the idea by now.

Summaries in Other Legal Documents

So far we have considered the kind of précis that should appear up front in analytical writing. But when it comes to the field that we call drafting — contracts, wills, trusts, statutes, rules, and the like — the summary will not capsulize

---

[11] *Kreager v. State Farm Mut. Auto. Ins. Co.*, 496 N.W.2d 346 (Mich. App. 1992).

the analysis because there is no analysis. Rather, the summary will take the form of an introduction or overview.

In a contract, for instance, the first paragraph (which is typically unnumbered) will identify the parties and the nature of the contract:

> This is a lease between McKinley Morganfield (Landlord) and Chester Burnett (Tenant) for the property at 123 Red Rooster Street. The parties agree as follows:

In addition, a long contract should have an informative table of contents. For that matter, any legal document that's longer than five or six pages will benefit from a table of contents.

In statutes, ordinances, and rules, the summary will take the form of a purpose clause. Reed Dickerson, the father of legal drafting in the United States, was skeptical about purpose clauses. He thought that most of them "wind up as pious incantations of little practical value because what little information they contain is usually inferable from the working text."[12] But plain-language experts disagree, believing as they do that most laws and legal documents should be drafted for an ordinary literate reader, and not just for judges and other lawyers. Here are two main reasons why: focusing on legal readers perversely ignores the very subjects of the law, the administrators and citizens it applies to; and by aiming to make the law clear to ordinary readers, skilled drafters will usually sharpen its meaning.[13]

One plain-language expert, Martin Cutts, has actually tested the value of purpose clauses. He rewrote an act of Parliament and included the following in his "Introduction":

---

[12] Reed Dickerson, *The Fundamentals of Legal Drafting* 286 (2d ed. 1986).
[13] *See* Bryan A. Garner, *Legal Writing in Plain English* 91 (2001) (setting out five reasons why it's wrongheaded to write only for legal experts); Law Reform Commn. of Victoria, *Plain English and the Law* 50 (1987; repr. 1990) ("The law should be drafted in such a way as to be intelligible, above all, to those directly affected by it. If it is intelligible to them, lawyers and judges should have no difficulty in understanding it and applying it.").

1.1   The main purposes of this Act are to give a
      customer:

(a)   the right to cancel a timeshare agreement or
      timeshare credit agreement; and

(b)   the right to receive information about the terms
      of the agreement.

The rest of this Act explains how and when these
rights apply.

1.2   This Act applies to a timeshare agreement or
      timeshare credit agreement if, when the agreement
      is being entered into, the customer, seller, or lender
      is in the United Kingdom or the agreement is to
      some extent governed by the law of the United
      Kingdom or a part of the United Kingdom.[14]

From his testing on law students, Cutts concluded that "an
introductory section, giving an overview of the main
purpose of the Act, is a great asset to readers (40% cited it
as a source of main points)."[15]

And that's not all. Cutts also included, at the end, a
"Citizen's Summary" of the Act's main substantive points.
This summary was labeled as not part of the Act and not to
be used by judges who interpret it. In the testing, 97% of
participants said that a Citizen's Summary should be
provided in every act of Parliament.[16]

That will be the day — when legislators and legislative
drafters, without fretting or finding reasons to avoid change,
take extra steps to make law clear to the people whose lives
it governs.

---

[14] Martin Cutts, *Lucid Law*, Clearer Timeshare Act at 3 (2d ed. 2000).

[15] *Id.* at 25.

[16] *Id.* at 27.

Final Thoughts on Opinions

In a judicial opinion with several issues, it may be difficult to summarize each one in the opening paragraphs. But with two or even three solid issues, you should be able to summarize in no more than four tight paragraphs, allowing one for the facts if you need it. The paragraphs do have to be tight, though. (Notice that my revised and meatier summaries of those Michigan opinions were shorter or only a mite longer than the originals.) At the very least, you can usually state all the deep issues, even if you can't answer each one except to say, for instance, that "we find no reversible error." At times, you can summarize selectively: "Rebennack raises four issues on appeal, two of which require careful review." And in any event, most cases do not involve more than a couple of weighty issues.

As you realize by now, I don't buy the notion that the summary must be only one or two paragraphs. Typically, it will be. But I don't object to several short paragraphs. Beyond that, though, the summary starts to become self-defeating. Garner says that, ideally, a deep issue should not exceed 75 words.[17] He of course means 75 words for *each issue*, including the answer.

I would not hesitate to call the summary just that, despite the traditional lack of a heading to begin opinions. Before I tested the revised *Wills* opinion, a colleague urged me to drop the heading, "Summary." Too radical, he said. Well, maybe. But if a business memo can have a heading like "Executive Summary," why can't an opinion have one too? Calling the opener a summary might even encourage writers to really summarize.

That leads to my last point — the value of the summary not just for the reader, but for the writer as well. It helps test the opinion. Although it appears first, it should be written last. More accurately, it should be completed and

---

[17] Garner, *supra* note 3, at 1, 5, 34–35.

polished last. Start with the issue part of the summary, but hold off on writing the answer part until the end. For how can you summarize your answer until you have worked through your analysis? You may eventually decide that your issue, too, needs refining — or deepening.

The summary, then, both shapes and reflects the analysis. The quality of the one affects the quality of the other. Of all the Michigan opinions cited earlier, the one that seemed to me the most slippery was *People v. Daoud*.[18] And I had the hardest time summarizing the answer. I'm not suggesting that summarizing is easy. But it's bound to be easier with a clear opinion. Bad summaries are a bad sign.

---

[18] 614 N.W.2d 152 (Mich. 2000).

The Straight Skinny on
Better Judicial Opinions
(Part 2)

In Part 1, I discussed my testing of the two opinions — the original published version and my revised version — that are reproduced on pages 25–34. Now I discuss the main differences between the opinions.

∾ ∾ ∾

I wrote the revised opinion in plain language. Please remember that "plain language" has become the established shorthand for a broad set of writing guidelines. I have identified more than 40 guidelines, contained in five categories: in general, design, organization, sentences, and words.[1] Only the uninformed and the misinformed think that plain language involves a handful of rudimentary techniques.

Of course, no one kind of legal document will call into play all the guidelines. In an opinion, for instance, a judge is not usually worried about minimizing definitions or making a table of contents or testing the document on a small group of typical users. At the same time, virtually all the changes I made in the revised opinion reflect plain-language guidelines.

---

[1] *The Elements of Plain Language*, this book at 69.

1. Begin the opinion with a good summary.

(*See First Things First: The Lost Art of Summarizing*, this book at 73.)

2. Divide the opinion into short sections (and subsections, as needed); use informative headings; begin each section with a summary.

These points are fairly self-explanatory. A quick comparison of the opinions (pages 25–34) will show that the original used no headings; the revised opinion used three, each followed by a summarizing paragraph.

3. Use topic sentences that advance the analysis.

The best topic sentences look backward and forward: they connect back to the point made in the previous paragraph, and they summarize the main point of the new paragraph. At their best, they combine to form an outline of the discussion or analysis.

If you think that topic sentences are overrated or beneath the dignity of adept writers, then you would have to conclude that they played no part in the clear preference for the revised opinion. Look over the difference between the topic sentences — the paragraph openers — and ask whether you would discount their importance. These are from the analytical part (not the facts and procedural history) of the two opinions.

Original:

Uninsured motorist coverage is not required by statute; thus, the contract of insurance determines under what circumstances the benefits will be awarded.

A "substantial physical nexus" between the unidentified vehicle and the object causing the injury to the insured has been found where the object in question was a *piece* of, or *projected* by, the unidentified vehicle, but not where the object originates from an occupant of an unidentified vehicle.

In *Hill, supra* at 384–385, the plaintiff's husband was driving his vehicle when a camper-truck passing in the opposite direction propelled a large rock through the car's windshield, causing the husband's death.

In the case at bar, the parties stipulated that there was no actual physical contact between plaintiff's automobile and the unidentified vehicle in question. Rather, the bullets fired by an occupant of the unidentified vehicle struck plaintiff's car.

Reversed and remanded for entry of summary disposition in favor of defendant.

Revised:

The controlling case is *Kreager v State Farm Mutual Automobile Ins Co*, 197 Mich App 577; 496 NW2d 346 (1992). The *Kreager* court distinguished between an object that comes from an occupant and an object that is projected by the unidentified vehicle itself.

Furthermore, the case that the trial court relied on, *Hill, supra*, is distinguishable.

The present case is like *Kreager*, not *Hill*: the projectile came from a gun fired by an occupant of the unidentified vehicle, not from the vehicle itself.

We reverse and remand for the entry of summary disposition in favor of defendant.

4. Omit unnecessary detail, including unnecessary cases.

Appendix B (page 99) contains a struck-through version of the original opinion. From that example, I think we can identify four main kinds of unnecessary detail.

First, statements of the obvious. For instance: "In 1994, defendant issued a policy of insurance to plaintiff to cover his 1989 Mercury Sable." Another instance: "Plaintiff subsequently [after the accident] filed a claim with defendant for medical and uninsured motorist benefits." Of course he did. We knew that from the start.

Second, needless repetition. For instance, the court cites the *Hill* case no fewer than three times for the rule that physical contact does not require direct physical contact.

Third, unnecessary facts. It makes no difference what kind of car Wills was driving or where he was driving it. Likewise, in the decisive *Kreager* case, it makes no difference why the insured was standing beside his car when he was shot at from the other car.

Fourth, unnecessary cases. This category may provoke a little more debate. The original opinion cites nine cases; the revised opinion cites four. More specifically, the original opinion cites four cases for the rule that physical contact can include indirect physical contact if the striking object was projected by the unidentified car. Then the court analyzes the *Kreager* case (the insured was shot while standing outside his car) and the *Hill* case (the insured was killed by a large rock that the other car propelled through his windshield). Then the court distinguishes *Hill*, provides three *see also* citations with parentheticals, and analogizes to the *Kreager* case. Essentially, the court sets out a rule with string citations, analyzes two of those cases, distinguishes *Hill* and three other cases, and analogizes to *Kreager*. This piling on of authority at different points requires the court to use multiple *supras*.

In contrast, the revised opinion starts with a summarizing paragraph that contains no citations; analyzes the controlling *Kreager* case; briefly analyzes the *Hill* case and cites one more recent case that was consistent with *Hill*; and explains that the present case is like *Kreager*, not *Hill*.

The question for opinion-writers is whether they should cite every case that has ever considered the issue. Or is it enough to deal only with the controlling case or cases? I'd say that writers should be judiciously selective. There's no need to analyze or even cite a line of cases that state essentially the same rule. Readers will not object to an occasional *see also* or a two-sentence analysis of a reinforcing case. But at some point, the opinion that seeks to be exhaustive will cease to be clear and effective.

5. Omit unnecessary words.

One of the all-time best quotations about writing appears in Wilson Follett's *Modern American Usage*:

> [T]o eliminate the vice of wordiness is to ensure the virtue of emphasis, which depends more on conciseness than on any other factor. Wherever we can make twenty-five words do the work of fifty, we halve the area in which looseness and disorganization can flourish, and by reducing the span of attention required we increase the force of the thought.[2]

I said earlier that the *Wills* case is not a terrible specimen or even a bad specimen. It's average, and it contains a typical assortment of faults. Wordy phrases, for instance: *has a duty to (must); injured as a result of (in) an automobile accident; enter judgment with regard to (on) the coverage dispute; rulings with regard to summary disposition motions (on summary-disposition motions); the court found in favor of (for) plaintiff; under what circumstances (when) the benefits will be awarded; in order to find coverage (for coverage).*

Notice how many of these examples involve an unnecessary *of*. More examples: *a policy of insurance (an insurance policy); as part of this policy (in this policy); the identities of the occupants (the occupants' identities); the contract of insurance (the insurance contract); was dispositive of the dispute (governed the dispute).*

Finally, beyond these recurring kinds of wordiness, you have the surplusage that is harder to categorize because it is so endlessly variable. It results from turning words into

---

[2]   Wilson Follett, *Modern American Usage* 14 (1966).

phrases and phrases into clauses, from overspecifying, from adding little unnecessary bits that are entirely clear from the context, from not seeing how a second reference to the same thing can be shortened, from pointless repetition — in short, from not having developed the writer's eye for tightening. Here are more examples from the two opinions. In each bullet, the original opinion is first and the revised opinion second:

- As part of this policy, defendant promised to pay plaintiff certain damages if he were injured as the result of an automobile accident between his vehicle and a vehicle driven by an uninsured motorist.

  State Farm's policy promised to pay Wills if he was injured in an accident between his vehicle and an uninsured motor vehicle.

- The parties agree that there was no actual physical contact between the unidentified automobile from which the shots were fired and plaintiff's automobile.

  There was no actual physical contact — no direct contact — between the two cars.

- The unidentified vehicle and its occupants left the scene of the accident, and the identities of the occupants remain unknown.

  The other car drove away, and its occupants are unknown.

- This Court has construed the physical contact requirement broadly to include indirect physical contact as long as a substantial physical nexus exists between the unidentified vehicle and the object cast off by that vehicle or the object that strikes the insured's vehicle. A "substantial physical nexus" between the unidentified vehicle and the object causing the injury to the insured has been found where the object in question was a *piece* of, or *projected* by, the unidentified vehicle, but not where the object originates from an occupant of an unidentified vehicle.

In cases involving indirect physical contact, this court
has required a "substantial physical nexus" between the
unidentified vehicle and the object that it casts off or the
object that strikes the policyholder's vehicle. But there
is no physical nexus when the striking object comes from
an occupant of the unidentified vehicle . . . .

- In the case at bar, the parties stipulated that there was no
actual physical contact between plaintiff's automobile
and the unidentified vehicle in question. Rather the
bullets fired by an occupant of the unidentified vehicle
struck plaintiff's car. . . . Thus, where it is undisputed
that an *occupant* of an unidentified vehicle moving
alongside plaintiff's vehicle shot at and hit plaintiff's
vehicle, i.e., the projectile here came from a gun, not
from the vehicle itself, plaintiff cannot show the requisite
substantial physical nexus between the unidentified
vehicle and himself or his vehicle. *Kreager, supra.*

The present case is like *Kreager*, not *Hill*: the projectile
came from a gun fired by an occupant of the unidentified
vehicle, not from the vehicle itself. Because Wills cannot
show a substantial physical nexus between the uninsured
vehicle and his vehicle, he is not entitled to benefits.

There is no easy or mechanical fix for a wordy style. The
only remedy is a heightened critical faculty. And the only
route to that is through training, reading, and critique —
along with a deep sympathy for the reader and an antipathy
toward clutter. Here is Wilson Follett again:

To make our words count for as much as possible is surely
the simplest as well as the hardest secret of style. Its
difficulty consists in the ceaseless pursuit of the thousand
ways of rectifying our mistakes, eliminating our
inaccuracies, and replacing our falsities — in a word,
editing our prose.[3]

---

[3] *Id.*

The greatest favor that appellate courts could do for themselves and their readers is to hire a few good editors — real editors, not just people who check citations, punctuation, and grammar. Of course, that would require enough humility to recognize that all writers, even the best ones, need editing.

6. Prefer short and medium-length sentences, and plain words.

Bryan Garner recommends, as a guideline, that writers keep their average sentence length to about 20 words.[4] Richard Wydick recommends an average of below 25 words.[5] So let's say that 20 words is an ideal average.

The original opinion averages 25 words (excluding citation sentences). The revised opinion averages 19.

As for inflated diction and legalese, the original opinion includes the following: *pursuant to, subsequently, instant case, originates from, case at bar, requisite.* You might argue that none of these are egregious or even high-toned, but I didn't use them in the revised opinion.

7. Avoid unnecessary citations; use the parties' names; punctuate well.

I'll end with a miscellany.

First, citations. In a couple of places, the original opinion uses string citations for undisputed points. Why do that? In another place, discussing the *Hill* case, it has a pinpoint citation to the facts in *Hill*. Why do that? In the discussion of *Hill*, it includes a pinpoint citation after every sentence. I would tend to save pinpoint cites for quotations and dispositive rules, especially if you are putting citations in

---

[4] Bryan A. Garner, *Legal Writing in Plain English* 19 (2001).
[5] Richard C. Wydick, *Plain English for Lawyers* 36 (5th ed. 2005).

the text instead of in footnotes.[6] Otherwise, the writing keeps getting interrupted by citation hiccups. See for yourself as you look over the original opinion.

Second, party names. I used the parties' names — Wills and State Farm — instead of "plaintiff" and "defendant." How many times, in reading opinions, have you had to stop and think who is the "plaintiff" or the "defendant"? Names are more vivid — they raise a picture in the reader's mind. We can at least be grateful that the original opinion did not use "appellant" and "appellee."

Finally, punctuation. Everyone should own *The Redbook*, by Bryan Garner, or *The Gregg Reference Manual*, by William Sabin. For my money, they are the best, and I regularly consult both of them. They agree on how to form the possessive of a singular that already ends in *s* — *Wills's claim*. Garner is somewhat more strict than Sabin in requiring hyphens with phrasal (compound) adjectives, and I agree that the following phrases in the original opinion should have used hyphens (which I'll now include): *uninsured-motorist provisions, uninsured-motorist benefits, declaratory-judgment action, summary-disposition motions, uninsured-motorist coverage, uninsured-motorist insurance carrier, phantom-vehicle claims, physical-contact requirement, substantial-physical-nexus requirement, uninsured-motor-vehicle coverage*. The hyphens help to avoid reader miscues, and the double hyphens may indicate a need to rephrase. As the very last point, note that the original opinion does not use a single dash. The revised opinion uses three. The handy and versatile dash belongs in every writer's punctuation kit. The notion that it's too informal for legal writing is silly.

---

[6] *Cf.* Bryan A. Garner, *The Citational Footnote*, 7 Scribes J. Legal Writing 97 (1998–2000) (recommending that citations — and citations only — appear in footnotes).

Conclusion

The message for opinion-writers is the same as for all legal writers. Care enough to work at your craft. Become critical-minded about words. Read the best books on writing. Pay attention to models. Keep at hand a group of current references on grammar and usage. Welcome good editing. Put yourself in your readers' shoes and resolve not to waste their time. Above all, revere clarity and simplicity — in a style that's straightforward and lean.

APPENDIX B
Omitting Unnecessary Detail

STATE OF MICHIGAN

COURT OF APPEALS

Robert Wills

      Plaintiff-Appellee,

v.

State Farm Insurance Company

      Defendant-Appellant.

Before: Judges A, B, and C.

JUDGE A

    Plaintiff Robert Wills filed a declaratory judgment action against defendant State Farm Insurance Company to determine whether defendant has a duty to pay benefits under the uninsured motorist provisions found in plaintiff's policy with defendant. ~~Pursuant to the parties' stipulated statement of facts,~~ [T]he trial court granted summary disposition in plaintiff's favor upon finding coverage where gunshots fired from an unidentified automobile passing plaintiff's vehicle caused plaintiff to drive off the road and suffer injuries. Defendant appeals as of right. We reverse and remand.

~~In 1994, defendant issued a policy of insurance to plaintiff to cover his 1989 Mercury Sable.~~ As part of [the] policy, defendant promised to pay plaintiff certain damages if he were injured as the result of an automobile accident between his vehicle and a vehicle driven by an uninsured motorist. The policy stated as follows:

> We will pay damages for *bodily injury* an *insured* is legally entitled to collect from the owner or driver of an *uninsured motor vehicle*. The *bodily injury* must be caused by [an] accident arising out of the operation, maintenance or use of an *uninsured motor vehicle*.
>
> *Uninsured Motor Vehicle* — means:
>
> * * *
>
> 2.   a "hit-and-run" land motor vehicle whose owner or driver remains unknown and which strikes
> a.   the *insured* or
> b.   the vehicle the *insured* is *occupying* and causes *bodily injury* to the *insured*. [Emphasis in original.]

While plaintiff was driving ~~his Sable on Shaw Lake Road~~ in Barry County, another vehicle pulled alongside his car as if it were passing him in the left lane. Suddenly, plaintiff saw a flash and heard gunshots. Reacting to the shots, plaintiff ducked down to the right ~~toward the floor of the passenger area to avoid injury.~~ Upon doing so, plaintiff turned the ~~Sable's~~ steering wheel to the right. The vehicle swerved off the road and hit two trees. As a result of the accident, plaintiff injured his neck and back, requiring surgery. The parties agree that there was no actual physical contact between the unidentified automobile from which the shots were fired and plaintiff's automobile. The unidentified vehicle and its occupants left the scene of the accident, and the identities of the occupants remain unknown.

~~Plaintiff subsequently filed a claim with defendant for medical and uninsured motorist benefits.~~ Defendant ~~paid plaintiff his medical benefits but~~ denied plaintiff's claim for uninsured motorist benefits because there was no physical contact between plaintiff's [car] and the unidentified vehicle. Plaintiff responded by filing a declaratory judgment action ~~asking the trial court to enter judgment in his favor with regard to the coverage dispute~~.

Defendant moved for summary disposition under MCR 2.116(C)(8) and (C)(10). At the hearing on defendant's motion, the trial court distinguished this Court's decision in *Kreager v State Farm Mutual Automobile Ins Co*, 197 Mich App 577; 496 NW2d 346 (1992), from the instant case and relied upon *Hill v Citizens Ins Co of America*, 157 Mich App 383; 403 NW2d 147 (1987), to find that a sufficient physical nexus existed between the two involved automobiles because, while they were moving, a projectile came from one car and entered the other. Therefore, the court found in favor of plaintiff under MCR 2.116(C)(8) and (C)(10) and denied defendant's motion.

We review de novo the trial court's rulings with regard to summary disposition motions, declaratory judgments, and questions of law. See ~~Cardinal Mooney High School v Michigan High School Athletic Ass'n, 437 Mich 75, 80; 467 NW2d 21 (1991);~~ *State Treasurer v Schuster*, 215 Mich App 347, 350; 547 NW2d 332 (1996)~~; Michigan Residential Care Ass'n v Dep't of Social Services, 207 Mich App 373, 375; 526 NW2d 9 (1994)~~.

~~Uninsured motorist coverage is not required by statute; thus, the contract of insurance determines under what circumstances the benefits will be awarded. Berry v State Farm Mutual Automobile Ins Co, 219 Mich App 340, 346;~~

~~556 NW2d 207 (1996); *Auto-Owners Ins Co v Harvey,*~~
~~219 Mich App 466, 470; 556 NW2d 517 (1996).~~ An
uninsured motorist policy's requirement of "physical
contact" between a hit-and-run vehicle and the insured or
the insured's vehicle is enforceable in Michigan. ~~*Berry, supra*~~
~~at 347;~~ *Kreager, supra* at 581–583; *Hill, supra* at 394. This
Court has construed the physical contact requirement
broadly to include indirect physical contact as long as a
substantial physical nexus exists between the unidentified
vehicle and the object cast off by that vehicle or the object
that strikes the insured's vehicle. *Id.*

A "substantial physical nexus" between the unidentified
vehicle and the object causing the injury to the insured has
been found where the object in question was a *piece* of, or
projected by, the unidentified vehicle, but not where the
object originates from an occupant of an unidentified
vehicle. See ~~*Berry, supra at 350;*~~ *Kreager, supra* at 579;
Adams v Zajac, 110 Mich App 522, 526–527; 313 NW2d
347 (1981). In *Kreager, supra,* an occupant of an unidentified
vehicle shot the insured while he stood outside the driver's
side of his vehicle. ~~He was standing there because someone~~
~~in the unidentified vehicle had thrown a bottle at his car,~~
~~and he responded by throwing the bottle back at the~~
~~unidentified vehicle. The shooting occurred in apparent~~
~~retaliation.~~ After determining that the "physical contact"
requirement was dispositive of the dispute ~~between the~~
~~insured and his uninsured motorist insurance carrier,~~ this
Court stated:

> Plaintiff's injuries lack a sufficient "physical nexus"
> with the unidentified vehicle. Unlike the plaintiff in *Hill,*
> *supra,* plaintiff was not injured by an object accidentally
> projected by the uninsured vehicle. Rather, the
> "projectile" involved [here] was a bullet fired from the
> handgun used by the assailant. There was no projection
> resulting from the vehicle itself. [*Kreager, supra* at 583.]

This Court found no "substantial physical nexus" between the insured or his vehicle and the unidentified vehicle. ~~It also agreed with defendant that the insured's injuries did not arise from any physical contact between the vehicles.~~ Thus, ~~in *Kreager, supra* at 582–583,~~ this Court held that the insured could not recover uninsured motorist benefits.

In *Hill, supra* at 384–385, the plaintiff's husband was driving his vehicle when a camper-truck passing in the opposite direction propelled a large rock through the car's windshield, causing the husband's death. ~~Upon reviewing various Michigan and out-of-state cases,~~ [T]his Court found that ~~direct physical contact between the uninsured vehicle and the insured was not required in order to find coverage. Id. at 390. Rather, because the parties agreed that a rock came through the windshield just as the other vehicle passed,~~ the plaintiff could "establish a substantial physical nexus between the disappearing vehicle and the object cast off or struck." *Id.* at 394. Moreover, this Court believed that requiring an insured to prove indirect contact would also foreclose the possibility of fraudulent phantom vehicle claims. ~~Id.~~ ~~"In summary, the overwhelming majority of jurisdictions hold that the 'physical contact' provision in uninsured motor vehicle coverage may be satisfied even though there is no direct contact between the disappearing vehicle and claimant or claimant's vehicle." Id.; see also Berry, supra at 347–348, 350.~~

In the case at bar, the parties stipulated that there was no actual physical contact between plaintiff's automobile and the unidentified vehicle in question. Rather, the bullets fired by an occupant of the unidentified vehicle struck plaintiff's car. Thus, unlike *Hill*, there was no physical contact between the involved vehicles and no projectile that the unidentified vehicle cast against plaintiff's car. See also *Berry* [*v State Farm Mutual Automobile Ins Co*, 219 Mich App 340, 343–350; 556 NW2d 207 (1996)] (scrap metal left in road after trailer full of scrap passed through area fifteen minutes before insured collided with it satisfied substantial physical nexus requirement); ~~Adams, supra at 526–527 (summary disposition for Secretary of State reversed where insured's vehicle went out of control after striking or swerving to avoid striking a truck tire and rim assembly left in the highway as the indirect physical contact between the involved vehicles was sufficient); Lord v Auto-Owners Ins Co, 22 Mich App 669, 672; 177 NW2d 653 (1970) (recovery permitted where a hit-and-run vehicle struck a second vehicle that in turn was propelled into the plaintiff's vehicle)~~. Indeed, as this Court recognized in *Kreager, supra* at 581, the shooting was not related to the assailant's use of a motor vehicle as a motor vehicle because "the shots could just as readily have been fired from a building, a parked car, a bicycle, or by a pedestrian." Thus, where it is undisputed that an *occupant* of an unidentified vehicle moving alongside plaintiff's vehicle shot at and hit plaintiff's vehicle, i.e., the projectile here came from a gun, not from the vehicle itself, plaintiff cannot show the requisite substantial physical nexus between the unidentified vehicle and himself or his vehicle. *Kreager, supra.*

Reversed and remanded for entry of summary disposition in favor of defendant. Defendant, being the prevailing party, may tax costs pursuant to MCR 7.219.

How to Mangle
Court Rules and Jury Instructions

On any list of the most important kinds of writing done by the legal profession, you would have to include court rules and jury instructions. They are the beginning and end of the process for doing business in our courts. Lawyers have to live by them, and some defendants may have to die by them.[1] And yet, not surprisingly, they are often infected by the same attitudes and practices that have brought legal writing to grief for four centuries.[2]

---

[1] *See, e.g.*, *Weeks v. Angelone*, 528 U.S. 225 (2000) (involving contextual ambiguity in death-penalty instructions: one half-sentence said jurors "may" impose death for an aggravating factor; the other half-sentence said they "shall" choose life imprisonment if the death penalty is not "justified," possibly suggesting that death is always justified by an aggravating factor); *Buchanan v. Angelone*, 522 U.S. 269 (1998) (the same as *Weeks*); *California v. Brown*, 479 U.S. 538 (1987) (involving syntactic ambiguity in death-penalty instructions: in the phrase "must not be swayed by mere sentiment, conjecture, sympathy, passion, prejudice, public opinion or public feeling," does *mere* modify *sympathy*?); *Free v. Peters*, 12 F.3d 700 (7th Cir. 1993) (involving possible juror confusion over the technical terms *aggravating factor* and *mitigating factor*, as demonstrated by an academic study of the instructions); *Gacy v. Welborn*, 994 F.2d 305 (7th Cir. 1993) (the same as *Free*); Peter M. Tiersma, *Legal Language* 235, 236 (1999) (noting at least ten capital cases in which jurors asked for clarification of *mitigating* or *aggravating*, and concluding that "there have probably been dozens of people who have been condemned to die by juries who poorly understood the legal principles that were supposed to guide their decision").

[2] *See* Appendix 1 to this book.

Jury instructions are notoriously incomprehensible to the public.[3] Court rules have not been empirically tested the way jury instructions have, but a glance at most of them will confirm their familiar murky style:

> Such examination shall be held within a reasonable time but in any event not later than 10 days following the initial appearance if the defendant is in custody and no later than 20 days if the defendant is not in custody, provided,

---

[3] *See, e.g.*, Amiram Elwork, Bruce D. Sales & James J. Alfini, *Making Jury Instructions Understandable* 45–46 (1982) (describing a study in which revising two different sets of jury instructions into plain language improved the level of comprehension from 51% and 65% to 80% on both sets); Ursula Bentele & William J. Bowers, *How Jurors Decide on Death: Guilt Is Overwhelming; Aggravation Requires Death; and Mitigation Is No Excuse*, 66 Brook. L. Rev. 1011, 1072, 1076 (2001) (describing a study in which about half the jurors who had imposed death sentences mistakenly believed that the death penalty was required for an aggravating factor, that a mitigating factor had to be proved beyond a reasonable doubt, and that all jurors had to agree on the mitigating factor); Shari Seidman Diamond & Judith N. Levi, *Improving Decisions on Death by Revising and Testing Jury Instructions*, 79 Judicature 224, 230 (1996) (describing a study in which revised instructions on mitigating factors led to substantially higher comprehension); Phoebe C. Ellsworth, *Are Twelve Heads Better Than One?*, 52 Law & Contemp. Probs. 205, 219 (1989) (describing a study of videotaped jury deliberations in which half of the jurors' references to the law were inaccurate); Geoffrey P. Kramer & Dorean M. Koenig, *Do Jurors Understand Criminal Jury Instructions? Analyzing the Results of the Michigan Juror Comprehension Project*, 23 U. Mich. J.L. Reform 401, 429 (1990) (concluding that the authors' study "supports a growing body of literature suggesting that jury instructions are often lost on jurors, and can sometimes even backfire"); Alan Reifman, Spencer M. Gusick & Phoebe C. Ellsworth, *Real Jurors' Understanding of the Law in Real Cases*, 16 Law & Hum. Behav. 539, 550 (1992) ("Overall, jurors . . . responded correctly to questions of law less than half the time."); Bradley Saxton, *How Well Do Jurors Understand Jury Instructions? A Field Test Using Real Juries and Real Trials in Wyoming*, 33 Land & Water L. Rev. 59, 86 (1998) (describing a broad study in which jurors were able to correctly answer 70% of the questions about civil and criminal instructions — a better result than in most studies).

> however, that the preliminary examination shall not be
> held if the defendant is indicted or if an information against
> the defendant is filed in district court before the date set
> for the preliminary examination.[4]

Is there any reason on earth to write a sentence like that?
Or like this?

> Failure by a party to raise defenses or objections or to
> make requests which must be made prior to trial, at the
> time set by the court pursuant to subdivision (c), or prior
> to any extension thereof made by the court, shall
> constitute waiver thereof, but the court for cause shown
> may grant relief from the waiver.[5]

Now for the good news: things are slowly but steadily
changing. The Standing Committee on Rules of Practice
and Procedure of the Judicial Conference of the United
States deserves a standing ovation for its decision to rewrite
federal rules. Its Advisory Committee on Rules of Appellate
Procedure rewrote those rules, and the Supreme Court
approved the new ones in 1998. More recently, the Advisory
Committee on Criminal Rules completed a three-year effort
to restyle those rules. They were approved by the Supreme
Court in April 2002. And the restyled Rules of Civil
Procedure were published for comment in February 2005.[6]
No doubt the final products are not perfect, but they are
much cleaner and clearer than the old versions of these
federal rules.

---

[4] Fed. R. Crim. P. 5(c) (the old version, as it read before the restyling
project on criminal rules that was completed in 2001 and approved by
the Supreme Court in April 2002).

[5] Fed. R. Crim. P. 12(f) (old version).

[6] Comm. on Rules of Practice and Procedure, *Preliminary Draft of
Proposed Style Revision of the Federal Rules of Civil Procedure*
(Feb. 2005) (available at http://www.uscourts.gov/rules/Prelim_
draft_proposed_pt1.pdf).

As for jury instructions, a few states have taken the needed plunge. California, Delaware, Minnesota, and Michigan have developed plain-English instructions.[7] On the federal side, the District Judges Association of the Sixth Circuit has written jury instructions designed to "state the law in an understandable way."[8]

Important revisory projects like these involve huge amounts of time and effort — most of it volunteered by judges, lawyers, and law professors. The success of a project will depend on having the right leadership, the right blend of personalities, the right kinds of expertise, and the right operating procedures. Having served as a writing consultant on four projects (Sixth Circuit Criminal Jury Instructions, Michigan Criminal Jury Instructions, Federal Criminal Rules, and Federal Civil Rules), I can at least offer some thoughts on expertise and operating procedures. Here, then, are some surefire ways to go *wrong*.

1. Do not adopt a drafting guide or a style guide.

No lawyer would argue law without citing authority. No lawyer would say, "I think the rule is such-and-such because

---

[7] Judicial Council of California, *Civil Jury Instructions* (2005 ed.) (available at http://www.courtinfo.ca.gov/reference/documents/civiljuryinst.pdf); Superior Court of Delaware, *Pattern Jury Instructions for Civil Practice* (2000 ed.) (available at http://courts.state.de.us/Jury%20Services/pdf/?patternjury_rev.pdf); Comm. on Jury Instruction Guides, Minnesota District Judges Assn., *Minnesota Jury Instruction Guides: Civil* (1999) (not available electronically); Standing Comm. on Standard Criminal Jury Instructions, State Bar of Michigan, *Michigan Criminal Jury Instructions* (2d ed. 1989–1991) (not available electronically); *see also* Peter Tiersma, *The Rocky Road to Legal Reform: Improving the Language of Jury Instructions*, 66 Brook. L. Rev. 1081, 1099–118 (2001) (describing the California work, especially on the criminal rules, which were approved by the Judicial Council in August 2005).

[8] Comm. on Pattern Criminal Jury Instructions, Sixth Circuit District Judges Assn., *Pattern Criminal Jury Instructions* vii (1991 ed.).

that's what I seem to remember from law school." But we are willing to do something quite like that — rely on half-remembered principles or on instinct — when it comes to writing.

No writer, let alone a committee, can be heedless of accepted guidelines and preferred usage. On countless matters, from formatting to handling conditions to using the serial comma, your committee needs to adopt a few reference sources. Otherwise, you are flying blind. True, even the experts may disagree on some matters, but the committee should not spend time discussing where to use hyphens or whether to write "a witness' testimony" or "a witness's testimony."

So what to use? For usage and style generally, the choice is easy: Bryan Garner's superb *Dictionary of Modern Legal Usage* (2d ed. 1995). More specifically, for court rules I'd also adopt Garner's *Guidelines for Drafting and Editing Court Rules*, a handy booklet published by the Administrative Office of the United States Courts. Every committee member should have it. There is nothing comparable for jury instructions, but a good starting point is Appendix A to the Federal Judicial Center's *Pattern Criminal Jury Instructions* (1988 ed.). Again, every committee member should have a copy. For greater depth, the drafter should probably be familiar with Elwork, Sales & Alfini's *Making Jury Instructions Understandable* (1982).

2. Do not use a writing expert.

Even with your adopted guides, your committee and reporter will still need the help of a writing expert. Naturally, I would say that, but operating without one is probably the worst mistake of all. Here's why.

First, no drafting guide is likely to be complete, to cover every question that may arise. A writing expert will have the answers in his or her head, or will know where to go for the answers. The expert will be steeped in *all* the literature on drafting.

Second, the writing expert will bring to the project a heightened concern for clarity and brevity. Committee members may sometimes lose sight of these goals in pursuit of substantive accuracy. All these goals are important, and in my opinion they are usually complementary.[9]

Third and most obvious, the writing expert will bring the experience and skill needed to achieve — or more closely approach — these goals. No matter how accomplished and knowledgeable the committee members and the reporter are, they are probably not schooled in drafting or editing. Their expertise lies in substantive law and in procedure, not in clear communication. A good lawyer does not a good drafter make.

An expert will turn a trained eye on inconsistencies and ambiguities, on sentence and paragraph thickets that need untangling, on inflated diction and wordiness, and even on grammatical blunders. Please get yourself one.

3. Ignore your adopted guides and your writing expert.

It's one thing to have good resources available; it's another thing to use them. It may seem too obvious for words that your committee should follow the guides it adopts and should trust its writing expert, but what's obvious is not always what's done.

Example: when an inconsistency was pointed out during a committee meeting, one member said, "I don't think we have to be consistent every time, with all the *t*'s crossed and *i*'s dotted the same way." Well, I'm sorry, but consistency is the cardinal rule of drafting. If you say *cannot* in one place

---

[9] *See* Carol Ann T. Mooney, *Simplification of the [Federal] Rules of [Appellate] Procedure*, 105 Dick. L. Rev. 237, 239 (2001) ("[T]he rewriting process inevitably uncovers ambiguities and, at least in the [federal] appellate rules . . . , ambiguities which had never been litigated and never been resolved.").

and *is unable to* in another, or if you aimlessly switch from *intent* to *intention* or from *adverse party* to *opposing party*, then you invite someone to puzzle over the difference — and perhaps try to make something out of it.

Or suppose you ignore the guideline to draft in the singular. Suppose you write that a party "must disclose in writing the names, addresses, and telephone numbers of the witnesses the party intends to rely on." If a witness has more than one telephone number, do they all have to be disclosed? (Change it to "the name, address, and telephone number of each witness.")

Your committee should have a good reason for departing from a drafting guideline. And it's not a good reason, usually, that a committee member thinks the different way "sounds better." Likewise, the committee should have a good reason for disregarding the writing expert. Of course, much of what he or she suggests may be style changes that have little consequence — individually. But a lot of little things add up. Clear writing, like a clean house, is not achieved in a few strokes. If your committee is not accepting 75% of the expert's edits, then the committee needs a new expert or a new attitude.

4. Use the writing expert late in the process.

As the committee's work proceeds, the committee becomes increasingly invested in what it has done and, on the flip side, less inclined to take another look at one part or another. So the writing expert who is brought in late will have to contend with inertia. Besides that, late use suggests that the expert is viewed as someone who deals in verbal cosmetics, someone who performs a kind of final inspection to smooth over the surface blemishes. In fact, the expert's work will always improve substantive accuracy and clarity.

The writing expert should be used early and often. If the committee is completely rewriting a set of court rules or jury instructions, the expert should do the first draft, then let the reporter have at it before it goes to the committee. The expert should mark those places where there may be a substantive question or an unintended change. If the committee is writing new or amended rules — a task that presumably requires substantive knowledge — the reporter should do the first draft and give it to the expert. One way or the other, the reporter and the expert should work closely together. That's the ideal.

5. Exaggerate the risk of change.

In these next two sections, I want to step back and encourage those who are contemplating a revisory project and reassure those who are engaged in one. Don't worry. Don't be tentative. Go ahead and transform that legalese. The potential benefits far outweigh the risk.

The risk, of course, is that you might unintentionally change meaning. It's a risk that lawyers grossly exaggerate. Let me illustrate with some examples from the style revision of the Federal Rules of Criminal Procedure. Ask yourself whether, in anyone's wildest imagination, we have changed the meaning.

- *Before*: in the absence of such consent by the defendant.[10]

  After: if the defendant does not consent.[11]

- *Before*: shall not utilize that grand jury material for any purpose other than assisting [X].[12]

  After: may use that information only to assist [X].[13]

- *Before*: This rule shall be in addition to and shall not supersede the authority of the court to issue appropriate protective orders . . . .[14]

---

[10] Fed. R. Crim. P. 5(c) (old version, before the restyling project).
[11] Fed. R. Crim. P. 5.1(d) (current, restyled version).
[12] Fed. R. Crim. P. 6(e)(3)(B) (old version).
[13] *Id.* (restyled version).
[14] Fed. R. Crim. P. 12.3(d) (old version).

After: This rule does not limit the court's authority to issue appropriate protective orders . . . .[15]

- *Before*: Nothing in this rule shall preclude the taking of a deposition, orally or upon written questions, or the use of a deposition, by agreement of the parties with the consent of the court.[16]

  After: The parties may by agreement take and use a deposition with the court's consent.[17]

- *Before*: An indictment shall not be dismissed on the ground that one or more members of the grand jury were not legally qualified if it appears from the record kept pursuant to subdivision (c) of this rule that 12 or more jurors, after deducting the number not legally qualified, concurred in finding the indictment.[18]

  After: The court must not dismiss the indictment on the ground that a grand juror was not legally qualified if the record shows that at least 12 qualified jurors concurred in the indictment.[19]

In most revisory projects, you can make changes like this repeatedly, in sentence after sentence.

Of all the possible dangers, the one that seems to worry us most is that we might change a term of art. But true terms of art, technical terms with a fairly precise meaning, are far less common than lawyers tend to think.[20] Granted, distinguishing between a term of art and a piece of jargon,

---

[15] *Id.* (restyled version).

[16] Fed. R. Crim. P. 15(g) (old version).

[17] Fed. R. Crim. P. 15(h) (restyled version).

[18] Fed. R. Crim. P. 6(b)(2) (old version).

[19] *Id.* (restyled version).

[20] *See* Robert W. Benson, *The End of Legalese: The Game Is Over*, 13 N.Y.U. Rev. L. & Soc. Change 519, 561 (1984–1985) ("a small island of true terms of art"); Stanley M. Johanson, *In Defense of Plain Language*, 3 Scribes J. Legal Writing 37, 39 (1992) ("the small subcategory comprising terms of art").

or lawyers' shorthand, can be difficult.[21] As a practical matter, though, the distinction either does not have to be made at all or should not normally create a problem.

In court rules addressed to lawyers, you would not need to replace *affidavit* with *sworn statement*. You would not need to change *nolo contendere* or *in camera* or *subpoena* or *peremptory challenge* or *mistrial* — whether you called them terms of art or jargon. (I'd call them jargon.) On the other hand, in jury instructions you would avoid most terms like that because they are probably jargon. In the rarer instance where you might have a term of art — *reasonable doubt, proximate cause, negligence* — you would try to carefully explain it to your lay audience.[22]

But the point remains that lawyers tend to exaggerate what counts as a term of art. They often resist changing mere inflated diction or eliminating redundancy. Professor Peter Tiersma, who serves on the California criminal-instructions task force, gives two examples: not changing *aids, facilitates, promotes, encourages, or instigates* (the commission of a crime) to *helps or encourages*; and not changing *harbors, conceals, or aids* (a principal in a felony) to *helps or hides*.[23]

At any rate, even if you never change anything that remotely looks like it might be a term of art, you can go right on making the kinds of improvements illustrated at the beginning of this section.

6. Slavishly follow the exact language of statutes and opinions.

As I just suggested, moving judges and lawyers off linguistic dead center is a challenge. And the ultimate challenge

---

[21] *See* Bryan A. Garner, *A Dictionary of Modern Legal Usage* 873 (2d ed. 1995) ("Many such questions [about terms of art] are debatable . . . .").

[22] *See* Tiersma, *supra* note 7, at 1101–07 (discussing how the criminal rules avoid some "technical terms" and define others).

[23] *Id.* at 1106–07, 1109.

is moving them off the language of statutes and opinions. Consider: "the Los Angeles judges say that jury instructions should repeat the law the way it exists, legalese or no legalese, and fear that altering words can change their legal meaning."[24] Yes, it can — but done right, it won't. What we need is good judgment, not blind fear.

Let me offer a few more examples, this time from a quick check in Volume 2 of the *Michigan Criminal Jury Instructions*:[25]

- *Statute*: [W]hether the defendant was driving at an immoderate rate of speed shall not depend upon the rate of speed fixed by law for operating such vehicle.[26]

  Jury instruction: Whether the defendant was driving at an unreasonable speed does not depend on the speed limit.[27]

- *Statute*: Any person who shall endeavor to incite or procure any person to commit the crime of perjury, though no perjury be committed, shall be guilty of a felony . . . .[28]

  Jury instruction: The defendant is charged with the crime of attempting to persuade another person to commit perjury.[29] [Note: Could you omit *the crime of*? Also, the instruction goes on to plainly set out the elements of the crime.]

---

[24] Caitlin Liu, *Say What, Your Honor?*, L.A. Times A26 (Sept. 7, 2000); *see also* Rosemary J. Park & Ruth M. Harvey, *Putting Jury Instructions in Plain English:* The Minnesota Jury Instruction Guides, Clarity No. 44, at 13, 16 (Dec. 1999) ("Some judges and lawyers felt that we must use the exact words and terms used in a law or in an appeals court opinion . . . .").

[25] *Supra* note 7.

[26] Mich. Comp. Laws Ann. § 750.326 (West 2004).

[27] Mich. Crim. Jury Instr. 16.19(1).

[28] Mich. Comp. Laws Ann. § 750.425 (West 2004).

[29] Mich. Crim. Jury Instr. 14.4(1).

- *Case*: [G]ross negligence [requires] . . . (3) The omission to use such care and diligence to avert the threatened danger when to the ordinary mind it must be apparent that the result is likely to prove disastrous to another.[30]

  Jury instruction: Third, that the defendant failed to use ordinary care to prevent injuring another when, to a reasonable person, it must have been apparent that the result was likely to be serious injury.[31] [Or: Third, that the defendant failed to use ordinary care to prevent injuring somebody else when a reasonable person would have known that a serious injury was likely.]

Any translation into plain language involves some risk — whether you are translating a term of art, a legal rule, or what should be an ordinary idea. And sometimes a committee will not take the risk. During the restyling of the federal criminal rules, for instance, I recommended changing this formulation in the old rules: "probable cause to believe that an offense has been committed and that the defendant has committed it."[32] My change: "probable cause to believe that the defendant committed an offense" (or "the offense charged"). Admittedly, this is important language. A colleague at my school told me: "Your suggestion is not illogical, but it goes against so many years of entrenched practice that it will never fly. The defense attorney wants the fact-finder to have to make both [?] decisions; it makes the fact-finder more careful."[33] He was right that my suggestion did not fly. But were his reasons — entrenched practice and two decisions — good reasons? Are there really two decisions?

---

[30] *People v. Rettelle*, 433 N.W.2d 401, 403 (Mich. App. 1988) (citations omitted).

[31] Mich. Crim. Jury Instr. 16.18(4).

[32] Fed. R. Crim. P. 4(a), 5.1(a), 58(d)(3).

[33] E-mail from Professor Ronald Bretz, Thomas M. Cooley Law School (Oct. 3, 2000) (on file with author).

One last example — and it may take the prize for not budging. The restyled criminal rules are still littered with the phrase *an attorney for the government*. Why not *a government attorney*? you might ask. Can't do it, because federal statutes use the former.[34] Never mind that the latter doesn't change the significant words. And never mind that the criminal rules, which actually define *an attorney for the government*, could just as easily have defined *a government attorney*.[35]

Let me summarize this section and the previous one with a list of bullets that may help to fortify reformers everywhere:

- In any project, most of the changes will involve the kind of basic style changes illustrated in the list on pages 112–13.
- The cumulative effect of those style changes will be a striking improvement in clarity.
- Where translation and risk may be involved, the committee can get it right, as many other groups have done.
- If we are paralyzed by the risk, nothing will change; our profession will be forever buried under mountains of legalese.
- In jury instructions, nothing could be more futile than sacrificing clarity. What is the point if jurors don't understand?
- If a revised jury instruction is disapproved on appeal, well, so are legalistic instructions often disapproved. And was the revised instruction disapproved just because of the new language, or was there an underlying fault in the original instruction?

---

[34] *E.g.*, 18 U.S.C. §§ 2516(3), 3127(5), 3552(d) (2000).

[35] *See* Fed. R. Crim. P. 54(c) (old version); 1(b)(1) (restyled version).

- Any mistakes the committee makes will be more than offset by the ambiguities and uncertainties that it uncovers and fixes — even apart from the overall improvement in clarity.

7. Ignore your audience.

Jury instructions are a unique form of legal writing. They don't involve legal analysis and argument as briefs and memos do. Yet they fit under the category of legal drafting — with statutes, rules, and contracts — only in a loose sense. Like statutes and court rules, they set out law, they form a self-contained whole, they are meant to govern conduct, and they are devoid of any writer's voice. But rather than creating law, they restate it. What's more, while statutes may have several audiences (courts, lawyers, administrators, the public) and court rules are addressed to judges and lawyers, jury instructions are directed primarily to a lay audience and, in most cases, are still delivered orally.

So jury instructions carry a heavier burden than almost any other form of communication you can think of: they deal with a fairly difficult subject that has to be understood by the public through listening to them all at once. They need to be as clear as humanly possible. They should be conversational. And they should do what may be unusual for other kinds of drafting. For instance:

- Address the jurors directly. (Not "one test that may be helpful" but "one test you can use.")
- Use first person for the judge. (Not "the court ruled that" but "I ruled that.")
- Use contractions.
- Use questions. ("To find the defendant guilty, you would have to answer 'yes' to two questions. First, . . . ? Second, . . . ?")
- Use controlled repetition. ("So again, the government must prove . . . ." "Let me remind you that . . . .")

- Similarly, state things in alternative ways, such as positively and negatively. ("In other words, ..." "This means that . . . ." "A person must take some affirmative steps to renounce or defeat the purpose of the conspiracy. This would include things like . . . . But some affirmative step is required. Just doing nothing, or just avoiding the other members, would not be enough.")

- Use signposting and summarizing techniques. ("Now I want to explain to you about . . . ." "One last point about . . . ." "What all this means is that . . . ." "So, to summarize, you must decide whether . . . .")

- Use language that is case-specific. ("As I explained to you earlier, the defendant, _____, is on trial here because the government has charged that [brief description of the crime]." "During the trial, you've heard the testimony of _____, who is described to us as an expert in _____.")

- Use concrete examples to illustrate how the law applies. ("If someone walked into the courtroom wearing a raincoat covered with drops of water and carrying a wet umbrella, that would be circumstantial evidence from which you could conclude that it was raining.")

Committees that write jury instructions should take two other steps to make them understandable. A committee should include one or two lay members. And it should spot-test its work on members of the public, with a target goal of, say, 75 to 80% comprehension overall.

8. Fail to see ambiguity.

To start, let's be sure about the distinction between vagueness and ambiguity. The distinction is fundamental to legal drafting and interpretation, although judges and lawyers are forever calling vague language ambiguous.

Vagueness presents uncertainty at the margins of application. We could apply the term *in good health* to most persons without much disagreement. But we would still have the in-between cases, say someone with high (itself vague!) cholesterol. Of course, some terms are more vague than others — *vehicle* as compared with *car*. But even *car* is vague; does it include the PT Cruiser or an SUV? In fact, all natural language is vague to some degree (a truth that seems lost on many a "textualist" or "strict constructionist").

In drafting, vagueness is both unavoidable and a potential benefit. It allows flexibility and spares the drafter from the impossible task of having to identify, and include or exclude, every conceivable particular. The goal is to arrive at the right degree of vagueness: not too vague or too specific. Thus, the drafter shapes vagueness according to the intended meaning. Suppose you want to collect a fee from cars, trucks, vans, SUVs, motorcycles, and the like. *Motor vehicle* is too broad if you don't want to include lawn tractors or golf carts. So maybe you say *a motor vehicle that is driven on the public roadways* (itself vague!). But that is too broad if you want to exclude farm tractors. So maybe you say *a motor vehicle that is normally* (vague) *driven on the public roadways* (vague). But what if you want to exclude commercial buses? Maybe you have to create an exception. And so on, depending on what you want to cover.

Here is a quick sampling of vague terms from the Federal Rules of Criminal Procedure: *unjustifiable expense, essential facts, reasonably available, with reasonable certainty, without unnecessary delay, suitable age and discretion, promptly, extraordinary circumstances, probable cause, good cause, hearing-impaired, unintentional, appropriate official, reasonable opportunity, if feasible, in the public interest.* These are from just the first six rules.

Ambiguity is different: it presents an either–or choice between alternative meanings. With ambiguity, you might as well flip a coin, although courts try to rationalize their choice. Ambiguity is always unintended, always avoidable, and always a sin — the worst sin in drafting. Good drafters have a sharp eye for it.

Perhaps the most common type of ambiguity is syntactic, and the most common syntactic ambiguity is caused by modifiers in a series (even a two-part series):

- Tall women and men. [Does *tall* modify *men*?]
- Men and women who are tall. [Does *who are tall* modify *men*?]

Below are some syntactic ambiguities in the old federal criminal rules or in the proposed style revision that was published for comment in August 2000, or in both.[36]

- participated in the same act or transaction or in the same series of acts or transactions constituting an offense or offenses.[37] [Does *constituting an offense or offenses* modify *the same act or transaction*?]
- a warrant returned unexecuted and not canceled or a summons returned unserved or a duplicate thereof.[38] [What does *thereof* refer to?]
- (B) advise the defendant personally in open court — or, for good cause, in camera — that the court may not follow the plea agreement; and
  (C) advise the defendant personally that if the plea is not withdrawn, the court may dispose of the case less favorably toward the defendant than the plea agreement contemplated.[39] [Should the *in open court* modifier in (B) apply to (C) as well?]

---

[36] August 2000 version: Comm. on Rules of Practice and Procedure, *Preliminary Draft of Proposed Style Revision of the Federal Rules of Criminal Procedure* (available at http://www.uscourts.gov/rules/archive.htm).

[37] Fed. R. Crim. P. 8(b) (old version and August 2000 version).

[38] Fed. R. Crim. P. 4(d)(4), 9(c)(2) (old version only).

[39] Fed. R. Crim. P. 11(c)(5) (August 2000 version only).

- any designated book, paper, document, record, recording, or other material not privileged.[40] [Does *not privileged* modify all the items in the series?]

- If . . . a party discovers additional evidence or material previously requested or ordered, which is subject to discovery or inspection . . . .[41] [Does the *which*-clause modify *additional evidence*?]

- a search warrant . . . for a search of property or for a person within the district.[42] [Does *within the district* modify *property*?]

- copy of the return, inventory, and all other related papers.[43] [Does *copy of* modify *all other related papers*?]

I think these ambiguities are fixed in the final, approved version of the restyled rules — the current Federal Rules of Criminal Procedure.[44]

9. Believe in myths.

I have written and written about the myths that bedevil any effort to convert legalese into plain language. But this is no time to give them a pass. They are persistent and pernicious. And by keeping us from reforming our strange talk, they create disrespect for lawyers and for law.

If only I could replace these bullets with a symbol for blank cartridges:

---

[40] Fed. R. Crim. P. 15(a) (old version and August 2000 version).

[41] Fed. R. Crim. P. 16(c) (old version only).

[42] Fed. R. Crim. P. 41(a) (old version only).

[43] Fed. R. Crim. P. 41(g) (old version, which did not use the word *related*); 41(h) (August 2000 version).

[44] For examples of ambiguities in the civil rules, see Joseph Kimble, *Guiding Principles for Restyling the Civil Rules*, in Comm. on Rules of Practice and Procedure, *Preliminary Draft of Proposed Style Revision of the Federal Rules of Civil Procedure* x, xvi–xvii (Feb. 2005) (available at http://www.uscourts.gov/rules/Prelim_draft_proposed_pt1.pdf) (reprinted in 84 Mich. B.J. 56 (Sept. 2005); 84 Mich. B.J. 52 (Oct. 2005)).

- Plain language means baby talk or dumbing down the language.
- Plain language is not precise or legally accurate.
- Plain language is just about simple words and short sentences.
- There is no hard evidence to show that readers prefer plain language or that plain language is more understandable or more persuasive than traditional legal style.

Not one of these is true.

10. Continue to graduate law students who are untrained in legal drafting.

The other big obstacle to change, besides the myths about plain language, is the state of legal-writing programs at the law schools. Although many schools have improved these programs in the last decade, many other schools continue to disrespect their programs and professors in one way or another — such as the number of required credit hours for legal writing or the salary and status of the professors.[45]

More specifically and just as shamefully, the schools have neglected legal drafting. According to the 2005 survey by

---

[45] Kristin Gerdy, Assn. of Legal Writing Directors & Legal Writing Inst., 2005 Survey Results 7 (Question 12), 47 (Question 65), 53–54 (Question 75) (released July 2005) (available at http://www.alwd.org) (indicating that most legal-writing directors and teachers make significantly less than other law professors, that more than 40% of the teachers are on one- or two-year contracts, and that most of the 178 schools surveyed require no more than four hours of legal writing); Susan P. Liemer & Jan M. Levine, *Legal Research and Writing: What Schools Are Doing, and Who Is Doing the Teaching (Three Years Later)*, 9 Scribes J. Legal Writing 113, 134–61 (2003–2004) (indicating that, in 2003, only 65 law schools of the 190 surveyed had at least one legal-writing teacher in a tenure-track position, that most of these people are directors of their programs, and that only 14 schools have all their full-time writing faculty on tenure track).

the Association of Legal Writing Directors and the Legal Writing Institute, only 15 or 20 of the 178 schools surveyed require legal drafting as a substantial part of their programs, although a majority do offer it in their elective writing courses.[46] Likewise, in an earlier survey of practicing lawyers designed to rate lawyering skills, only about 20% of 1,200 lawyers thought that enough attention was given to drafting documents in law school — one of the lowest numbers for all the lawyering skills surveyed.[47] In addition, legal drafting showed the largest gap between what, in the lawyers' opinion, the law schools can effectively teach and what they do teach.[48]

But now comes an incongruity — actually, two of them. First, despite these numbers, most lawyers apparently regard themselves as quite good at drafting. Second, they regard the drafting done by all other lawyers as below par. So says Bryan Garner, who for years has informally surveyed lawyers at his seminars. Remarkably, 95% of them would claim to produce high-quality drafting, but only 5% of the documents they see are well drafted.[49] That's not what you'd call a formula for change.

As long as law schools continue to neglect drafting and as long as lawyers have no sense of their own deficiencies, then most court rules and jury instructions will stay mangled.

---

[46] Gerdy, *supra* note 45, at 11 (Question 20), 20 (Question 33), 21–22 (Question 35).

[47] Bryant G. Garth & Joanne Martin, *Law Schools and the Construction of Competence*, 43 J. Legal Educ. 469, 479, 481 (1993).

[48] *Id.* at 478.

[49] Bryan A. Garner, *President's Letter*, The Scrivener (newsletter of Scribes — Am. Socy. of Writers on Legal Subjects) 1, 3 (Winter 1998).

How to Write
an Impeachment Order

Obtuse, archaic, and verbose legal language ... is surely
even today a major reason for antipathy toward the legal
profession.
— Peter M. Tiersma[1]

If lawyers everywhere adopted this goal [of writing in
plain language], the world would probably change in
dramatic ways.
— Bryan A. Garner[2]

Let's hope that the next presidential impeachment does not
happen for at least another 130 years, if at all. By then, you
and I will hardly care, unless the genetic research into
prolonging life has paid off for us in miraculous ways. So
I don't expect to ever see my suggestions find their way
into an order on articles of impeachment. I offer them to
posterity — and to current judges who might find them
generally useful in writing orders of any type.

You may have noticed that during the Clinton
proceedings the administrators sometimes rooted around
in the Andrew Johnson impeachment for procedural and
linguistic precedent. Of course, lawyers tend to do that —
follow the old forms — which is one reason why legal
writing has been so bad for so long. Chalk it up to habit and

---

[1] Peter M. Tiersma, *Legal Language* 42 (1999).
[2] Bryan A. Garner, *A Dictionary of Modern Legal Usage* 661 (2d ed.
1995).

inertia, proclivities that are all too human. But please don't believe that just because a form has been around a long time, it must be tried and true. We greatly exaggerate the extent to which legal terms have been settled or fixed by precedent.[3] And no amount of precedent can justify the syntax, sentence length, verbosity, organization, and design of traditional forms and "models."

Judicial orders are a perfect example. They don't *have to* be written the way they usually are, they don't *have to* be stilted, but they usually are because that's the traditional style. Few writers will break free.

At any rate, it will probably happen that the administrators of the next impeachment trial will look to this last one. Regardless of the outcome, they'll find the orders below. (Think of looking for food and finding a very old sandwich.) Perhaps — not likely, but perhaps — some future scholar will also find this article and my suggested rewording. Then the administrators, including the presiding Chief Justice, will at least have a choice between legalese and plain language. No doubt they will be grateful for this good fortune and will enter my name into the *Congressional Record*. Ah, posthumous fame.

But I'd happily settle for less. I hope some judges will read this article — as well as some lawyers who prepare orders for judges to sign — and our profession will dump a little legalese as it sails along in the new millennium. I hope some judges will make it known that they want orders to be written in the new, the modern, the plain style. If judges will only lead the way, lawyers will follow. And I can't think of an easier starting point than orders.

---

[3] *See The Great Myth That Plain Language Is Not Precise*, this book at 37, 45 n. 7.

The Orders on the Articles of Impeachment

Here's the main order that ended the impeachment trial:

> The Senate, having tried William Jefferson Clinton, President of the United States, upon two articles of impeachment exhibited against him by the House of Representatives, and two-thirds of the Senators present not having found him guilty of the charges contained therein: it is, therefore, ordered and adjudged that the said William Jefferson Clinton be, and he is hereby, acquitted of the charges in this said article [these said articles?].[4]

Notice some of the familiar characteristics of legalese — even in just this one sentence:

- The sentence is too long. You might argue that the colon provides a break, but the colon is incorrect because the first half of the sentence won't stand as an independent clause. The colon should be a comma. (And the comma after *The Senate* should go.)

- The sentence is contorted. It begins with two long clauses (so-called absolute clauses): *The Senate, having tried . . . , and two-thirds of the Senators present not having found . . . .* And each of those two clauses has a reduced internal, or embedded, clause: *[that are] exhibited against him* and *[that are] contained therein.* Then, finally, we get the independent clause: *it is, therefore, ordered . . . .* Linguists call this kind of sentence "left-branching" because readers have to fight through incidental branches of meaning before getting to the main point in the independent clause, the linguistic trunk.[5] This structure is all too common in legal writing: *If . . . and if . . . and if . . . , then Pierce may . . . .* No good.

---

[4]   145 Cong. Rec. S1459 (daily ed. Feb. 12, 1999).

[5]   *See* Bryan A. Garner, *Securities Disclosure in Plain English* 53–56 (1999).

Readers would rather see the main subject and verb early on. Sometimes the remedy is to put multiple items, such as conditions or rules, in a list at the end of the sentence — so that it branches right. Sometimes the remedy is to convert to more than one sentence.

- We get an odd negative: *two-thirds of the Senators present not having found him guilty.*

- We get inflated words: *upon* instead of *on*, and *exhibited* instead of *brought.*

- We get one of our beloved doublets: *ordered and adjudged.*

- We get two of the worst antique words: *hereby* and *said* (in place of *the, this,* or *those*). Look at the two uses of *said*: *the said William Jefferson Clinton* and *this said article.* The said *said*s are as useless as lipstick on a carp. What in the world impels us to talk like this? Why not go all the way and make it *the said Senators*?

- We get other unnecessary words: *contained therein* and *in this said article.* There are no other charges in sight except the charges in the articles of impeachment. This is the kind of overprecision, or false precision, that is so often put forward to rationalize legalistic writing.

Here's an alternative. Which one do you vote for?

The Senate has tried William Jefferson Clinton, President of the United States, on two articles of impeachment brought by the House of Representatives. Fewer than two-thirds of the Senators present have found him guilty of those charges. It is therefore ordered that he is acquitted.

Or you could whittle down that version even further:

After a trial on two articles of impeachment against the President, William Jefferson Clinton, fewer than two-thirds of the Senators present have found him guilty. He is therefore acquitted.

Now, the proceedings were not yet formally completed. One last order had to be entered:

> Ordered, that the Secretary be directed to communicate to the Secretary of State, as provided in Rule XXIII of the Rules of Procedure and Practice in the Senate when sitting on impeachment trials, and also to the House of Representatives, the judgment of the Senate in the case of William Jefferson Clinton, and transmit a certified copy of the judgment to each.[6]

Thus were listeners and readers treated to a few more characteristics of legalese:

- The sentence is again long and contorted. The main trouble here is the big gap between the infinitive verb form (*to communicate*) and the object (*the judgment*). Good writers try to keep the subject, verb, and object fairly close together.[7]

- We get needless complexity, or so it seems. The Secretary is directed to communicate the judgment and to transmit a certified copy of the judgment. But isn't that all one operation? Presumably the Secretary does not phone in the judgment and follow with a certified copy.

- We get unnecessary information: "as provided in Rule XXIII of the Rules of Procedure and Practice in the Senate when sitting on impeachment trials." Would a federal judge write, "It is ordered that the motion for summary judgment is granted and the complaint is dismissed, as provided in Federal Rule of Civil Procedure 56(b)"? If the reference to the Senate's rules has to stay, it could be relegated to parentheses.

---

[6] Cong. Rec., *supra* note 4.
[7] *See* Bryan A. Garner, *The Winning Brief* 199–201 (2d ed. 2004); Richard C. Wydick, *Plain English for Lawyers* 41–43 (5th ed. 2005).

- We get unnecessary prepositional phrases: *the judg-ment of the Senate* instead of *the Senate's judgment*; and *in the case of William Jefferson Clinton* instead of *in this case*. Besides, we know what case it is by now.

- For good measure, we get roman numerals: *Rule XXIII*.

Here's an alternative:

> It is ordered that the Secretary send a certified copy of the Senate's judgment to the Secretary of State (as provided in Rule 23 of the Senate's rules in impeachment trials) and also to the House of Representatives.

Or if it's really necessary to communicate the judgment and also transmit a certified copy, then a list would work nicely:

> It is ordered that the Secretary:
>
> (1) communicate the Senate's judgment to the Secretary of State (as provided in Rule 23 of the Senate's rules in impeachment trials);
>
> (2) communicate the judgment to the House of Representatives; and
>
> (3) send a certified copy of the judgment to both.

One More Example

Let's take another example, this one from Irwin Alterman's excellent book on writing court papers.[8] As you can see, I'm not alone in thinking that court orders contain "an unbelievable amount of gibberish."[9] Alterman says that orders "confirm Mellinkoff's statement that some legal writing is not written for anyone; it is written just to be

---

[8] Irwin Alterman, *Plain and Accurate Style in Court Papers* 84–87, originally published in 2 Thomas M. Cooley L. Rev. 243, 291–93 (1984).

[9] *Id.* at 84.

written."[10] Below, without interruption, is one of Alterman's examples and his comments on the example. (Incidentally, the introductory matter, before the order itself, he calls "recitals.")

Traditional Style:

> Defendant having filed a motion for summary judgment, the plaintiff having filed a brief in opposition thereto, the matter having come on for hearing, the court being fully advised in the premises, and the court having denied the motion, now therefore
>
> It is hereby ordered . . . .

Suggested Style:

> Defendant moved for summary judgment. The parties filed briefs and the court heard argument. The court decided to deny the motion for the reasons stated in the bench opinion (or written opinion) of _____, _____.
>
> It is [therefore] ordered:
>
> (1)
> (2)
> (3)

Alterman's Comments:

- The suggested form is not one long assemblage of *having*-clauses.
- The form omits *the court being fully advised in the premises*, which is self-serving nonsense.
- The form does not try to summarize the court's reasoning.
- The form avoids the redundant *ordered, adjudged, and decreed.*

---

[10] *Id.* (paraphrasing David Mellinkoff, *Legal Writing: Sense and Nonsense* 65 (1982)).

But Where's the Dignity?

I can hear the response. Some will argue that formal acts deserve formal language — and that plain English is not suitable for the solemn and weighty matter of a judicial order, let alone an order on articles of impeachment. The answer to that is twofold.

First, formality is a dangerous thing; it often degenerates into pomposity. A writer can get away with saying *transmit* instead of *send*, or with the occasional extra word or longish sentence. But when you are persistently formal and long, you wind up with the kind of writing in the three orders we just looked at. Certainly, no one will claim — will they? — that those orders are eloquent, elegant, or poetic.

Second, I submit to you that the suggested alternatives are not undignified or even informal. They are simple and straightforward, the way an order should be. The notion that plain language is drab and undignified is one of the great myths — along with the myth that it's usually at odds with settled precedent, the myth that it's not precise, the myth that it's child's play, and the myth that it's only about short sentences and short words. Plain language is, if anything, more precise than traditional legal writing; it takes hard work and embraces a wide range of principles; it can be forceful and literary; and it's fitting for any occasion. Plain English is the American idiom.

So Who Cares?

After all this, you may be thinking, What's the big deal? Nobody (except fussbudgety writing teachers) complains about court orders. They don't cause any trouble. They are just a short instruction that embodies a previous decision or result. They have minimal content. Their style is not important.

Well, I say that habits of mind are important. The intractability and incremental growth of forms (they never get shorter) is important. The compelling evidence that lawyers overrate traditional style — and that plain language is decidedly more clear and effective — is important.[11] The myths about plain language are important. A dismissive attitude toward plain language is important.[12] The public's attitude toward our profession is important. The constant criticism, the ridicule, the parodies of legal style — centuries of it — is important.[13] And a willingness to learn and change is important.

So I say that the style of *every* piece of legal writing is important because, as Blake wrote, it lets us "see a World in a Grain of Sand."[14] Every piece of legalese reflects on the state of our professional currency, our language.

How do you write an impeachment order? The same way you should write any legal sentence, paragraph, page, or document. In plain language.

---

[11] *See Answering the Critics of Plain Language*, 5 Scribes J. Legal Writing 51 (1994–1995); *Writing for Dollars, Writing to Please*, 6 Scribes J. Legal Writing 1 (1996–1997).

[12] *See, e.g.*, George Hathaway, *A Plain English Lawyer's Oath* (Part 2), 78 Mich. B.J. 64, 66 (1999) (noting the Michigan Supreme Court's rejection of a plain-English lawyer's oath even as an *optional* alternative to the current oath).

[13] *See* Robert Eagleson, *Plain Language: Changing the Lawyer's Image and Goals*, 7 Scribes J. Legal Writing 119 (1998–2000).

[14] From the poem "Auguries of Innocence."

A Crack at Federal Drafting

This will not be the first or last article that criticizes the style of drafting in federal statutes. But it will, I believe, be different in at least one respect: it will scrutinize the style in just one small slice of federal drafting in a way that should edify drafters of any legal document. In fact, this inspection should open the eyes of all legal writers — for I'll identify some of the persistent, inexcusable failings that pervade all legal writing. I've done this kind of thing before, using the final orders from the Clinton impeachment trial.[1] If you think those impeachment orders were revealing, wait until you see the USA Patriot Act.[2]

It's amazing, really, how much you can wring out of a few paragraphs. And I'm not talking about subtle or arguable points; I'm talking about the kinds of changes that good stylists or editors would make almost routinely. At the same time, none of the items that I list below are what you would call major. None of them go to the unfriendly format of federal statutes or their overdivided structure. Nor do I get into organization or degree of detail. Nor do I raise the standard complaint about serpentine sentences full of embedded clauses, or even mention the passive voice. Individually, my changes may seem small, but taken as a whole, their effect is considerable. And so it is with writing: clarity does not come in one or two strokes, but through

---

[1] *See How to Write an Impeachment Order*, this book at 125; *see also The Lessons of One Example*, this book at 145.

[2] *Uniting and Strengthening America by Providing Appropriate Tools Required to Intercept and Obstruct Terrorism Act (USA Patriot Act) of 2001*, Pub. L. No. 107–56, 115 Stat. 272 (2001).

the cumulative effect of many improvements, some of them larger and some smaller.

How did our profession ever arrive at this state of linguistic distress? Apparently, 400 years' worth of legalese has left us blind. We are so used to it that we can't see it for what it is, or can't muster the will to resist, or don't care. The great irony is that most lawyers seem to consider themselves quite proficient at writing and drafting. They are deluded. But as Reed Dickerson, the father of American drafting, observed, "It is hard to sell people new clothes if they consider themselves already well accoutered."[3]

Of course, we all realize that legislative drafters work under pressure, that very often or perhaps most often they do not have a free hand, that the process is messy and variable, and that some drafters are no doubt skilled and experienced. Yet they are still heirs to "a history of wretched writing."[4] So it's not surprising that the habits I criticize have seemingly become ingrained.

At any rate, let me say a word about the paragraphs I'll use from the Patriot Act. I didn't scour the Act for the worst examples. I didn't scour the Act at all. These paragraphs came to my attention because they affect the Federal Rules of Criminal Procedure, which I have an interest in. The Advisory Committee on Criminal Rules spent three years between 1998 and 2001 restyling all the criminal rules — a huge undertaking — and I served as a consultant during the last part of the project. The restyled criminal rules were submitted to the Supreme Court in November 2001. At about the same time, Congress passed the Patriot Act, and the advisory committee had to scramble to insert conforming language into the new version of the rules. The Act amended Rules 6(e)(3)(C) and 41(a) of the old rules; the committee inserted the changes into 6(e)(3)(D) and 41(b)(3) of the new

[3] Reed Dickerson, *The Fundamentals of Legal Drafting* 2 (2d ed. 1986).
[4] Bryan A. Garner, *The Elements of Legal Style* 2 (2d ed. 2002).

rules. I'm going to deal only with the Rule 6 changes because the Rule 41 changes were much shorter.

Now, the committee decided that it had to use the statutory language in the court rules — an understandable decision but a serious setback for good drafting.[5] It's disheartening, after the long effort to improve the rules' clarity and consistency, to see that statutory language imported almost verbatim.

And here it is, in all its glory.

The Paragraphs That Affect Criminal Rule 6

This is from Title II, section 203(a)(1), of the Patriot Act:

Rule 6(e)(3)(C) of the Federal Rules of Criminal Procedure is amended to read as follows:

"(C)(i) Disclosure otherwise prohibited by this rule of matters occurring before the grand jury may also be made —

. . .

"(V) when the matters involve foreign intelligence or counterintelligence (as defined in section 3 of the National Security Act of 1947 (50 U.S.C. 401a)), or foreign intelligence information (as defined in clause (iv) of this subparagraph), to any Federal law enforcement, intelligence, protective, immigration, national defense, or national security official in order to assist the official receiving that information in the performance of his official duties.

. . .

---

[5] *See How to Mangle Court Rules and Jury Instructions*, this book at 105, 114–18.

"(iii) Any Federal official to whom information is disclosed pursuant to clause (i)(V) of this subparagraph may use that information only as necessary in the conduct of that person's official duties subject to any limitations on the unauthorized disclosure of such information. Within a reasonable time after such disclosure, an attorney for the government shall file under seal a notice with the court stating the fact that such information was disclosed and the departments, agencies, or entities to which the disclosure was made.

"(iv) In clause (i)(V) of this subparagraph, the term 'foreign intelligence information' means —

  "(I) information, whether or not concerning a United States person, that relates to the ability of the United States to protect against —

    "(aa) actual or potential attack or other grave hostile acts of a foreign power or an agent of a foreign power;

    "(bb) sabotage or international terrorism by a foreign power or an agent of a foreign power; or

    "(cc) clandestine intelligence activities by an intelligence service or network of a foreign power or by an agent of [a] foreign power; or

  "(II) information, whether or not concerning a United States person, with respect to a foreign power or foreign territory that relates to —

    "(aa) the national defense or the security of the United States; or

    "(bb) the conduct of the foreign affairs of the United States."

So What's the Trouble?

Did those paragraphs seem pretty normal — about par for legal drafting? I suspect they did, so let me try to identify some deficiencies. After each item, I'll include one or more examples, along with a revised version or a question.

1. *An Aversion to Pronouns*

   • "acts of a foreign power or an agent of a foreign power"

     acts by a foreign power or its agent

   • "the national defense or the security of the United States; or the conduct of the foreign affairs of the United States"

     ... or the conduct of its foreign affairs

2. *An Aversion to Possessives*

   • "clandestine intelligence activities by an intelligence service or network of a foreign power or by an agent of [a] foreign power"

     clandestine intelligence activities by a foreign power's intelligence service, intelligence network, or agent

3. *An Aversion to -ing Forms (Participles and Gerunds)*

   • "in the performance of his official duties"

     in performing his official duties

   • "in the conduct of that person's official duties"

     in conducting [or "to conduct"] that person's official duties

4. *An Aversion to Hyphens*

   • "foreign intelligence information"

     foreign-intelligence information

- "Federal law enforcement, . . . national defense, or national security official"

  Federal law-enforcement, . . . national-defense, or national-security official

5. *Overuse of "Such," "That" (as a Demonstrative Adjective), and "Any"*

- "~~Any~~ [A] Federal official to whom information is disclosed pursuant to clause (i)(V) of this subparagraph may use ~~that~~ [the] information only as necessary in the conduct of that person's official duties subject to any limitations on the unauthorized disclosure of ~~such~~ [the] information. Within a reasonable time after ~~such~~ disclosure, an attorney for the government shall file under seal a notice with the court stating the fact that ~~such~~ [the] information was disclosed . . . ."

6. *Cumbersome and Unnecessary Cross-References*

- "foreign intelligence information (as defined in clause (iv) of this subparagraph)"

  foreign-intelligence information (as defined in (C)(iv))

- "In clause (i)(V) of this subparagraph, the term 'foreign intelligence information' means — "

  "Foreign-intelligence information" means — [There's no need for the cross-reference, since the earlier provision, where the term was used, already referred forward to this part.]

7. *A Tendency Toward Syntactic Ambiguity*

- "foreign intelligence or counterintelligence (as defined in . . . 50 U.S.C. 401a)" [Does the parenthetical element modify both items? Yes?]

- "any Federal law enforcement, intelligence, protective, immigration, national defense, or national security official" [How many items does *Federal* modify? All of them?]

- "activities by an intelligence service or network of a foreign power" [Does *intelligence* also modify *network*?]

8. *General Wordiness*

- "in order to assist the official receiving that information in the performance of his official duties"

  for use in performing the official's duties

- "Any Federal official to whom information is disclosed pursuant to clause (i)(V) of this subparagraph may use that information only as necessary in the conduct of that person's official duties subject to any limitations on the unauthorized disclosure of such information."

  A federal official who receives information under (C)(i)(V) [or "receives grand-jury information"] may use it only as necessary to perform official duties [and?] subject to any limitations on its unauthorized disclosure.

- "Within a reasonable time after such disclosure, an attorney for the government shall file under seal a notice with the court stating the fact that such information was disclosed and the departments, agencies, or entities to which the disclosure was made." [But isn't the disclosure to an official, not an agency?]

  Within a reasonable time after disclosure, a government attorney must file, under seal, a notice with the court stating what information was disclosed and to whom [or "stating what information was disclosed, the federal official's name, and the official's agency"].

9. *General Fuzziness*

- "any Federal ... protective ... official" [?]
- "a United States person" [?]

10. *Needless Repetition*

After (C)(i)(V) requires that the disclosure be to assist the
official in performing official duties, (C)(iii) then requires
that the use be necessary in conducting official duties. I
kept both requirements in my redraft below, but I think the
first one — concerning the purpose for disclosure — could
probably go. Having to file a notice of the disclosure makes
it unlikely that someone will disclose for inappropriate
reasons.

(Incidentally, why the switch in these two provisions
from *in the performance of* (official duties) to *in the conduct
of*? What possible difference is there? Probably none, but
the switch creates a hint of contextual ambiguity.)

A Redraft

I'll leave it to you to decide whether the original or the following redraft is better. Just two comments: the only part I
reorganized is (C)(iv); and if I inadvertently changed a
meaning somewhere, it can easily be restored without
reverting to the style of the original. All right, then:

> Rule 6(e)(3)(C) of the Federal Rules of Criminal
> Procedure is amended to read as follows:
>
> (C)(i) Disclosure of a grand-jury matter may also be
> made:
>
> .   .   .
>
> (V) to a federal official who is engaged in law
> enforcement, intelligence, protection [?],
> immigration, national defense, or national
> security, if the matter involves foreign
> intelligence or counterintelligence (as they are
> defined in 50 U.S.C. 401a) or foreign-
> intelligence information (as defined in (C)(iv))
> and if the information is for use in perform-
> ing the official's duties.
>
> .   .   .

   (iii)   A federal official who receives grand-jury information may use it only as necessary to perform [his or her?] official duties and subject to any limitations on its unauthorized disclosure. Within a reasonable time after disclosure, a government attorney must file, under seal, a notice with the court stating what information was disclosed and to whom.

   (iv)   "Foreign-intelligence information" means any information about a person, a foreign power, or a foreign territory that relates to the national defense or the security of the United States, or to the conduct of its foreign affairs. The term includes any information about:

       (I)   the ability of the United States to protect against actual attack, potential attack, sabotage, international terrorism, or other grave hostile act by a foreign power or its agent; or

      (II)   clandestine intelligence activities by a foreign power's intelligence service, intelligence network, or agent.

Conclusion

Lawyers draft poorly. And for that to change, several related things must happen.

First, their loyal critics must keep complaining, keep agitating; I'll do my best, as a public service.

Second, reformers must keep exposing the myths about writing clearly, in plain language — like the myth that plain language is not precise, or involves just a few simple guidelines, or is not supported by any convincing evidence of its effectiveness.

Third, to overcome resistance and doubt, reformers must keep pointing to major advancements — like the restyled Federal Rules of Appellate, Criminal, and Civil Procedure, new article 9 of the UCC, and some of the work done by the Securities and Exchange Commission in the late 1990s.[6] The drafting in these projects may not be perfect, but compare it with what went before.

Fourth, lawyers must stop making excuses for traditional legal style and stop aping old models. This will require, to begin with, some humility and open-mindedness, and then a close encounter with some books on legal writing or a CLE course or a good editor. Like any other skill, writing well takes sustained effort; it's not innate.

Finally, law schools must end their shameful neglect of legal drafting. Although many schools have strengthened their writing programs in the last decade, those programs concentrate mainly on briefs and memos, not on drafting (contracts, wills, bylaws, statutes, rules). True, most schools do offer an elective in legal drafting, but only a small number — maybe 15 or 20 schools — require it as a substantial part of their writing programs.[7] It's no wonder, then, that most lawyers, steeped as they are in old forms and models, consider themselves good drafters. Nobody has ever shown them a better way.

---

[6] *See* Div. of Corp. Finance, U.S. Sec. & Exch. Commn., *Before & After Plain English Examples and Sample Analyses* (1998).

[7] Kristin Gerdy, Assn. of Legal Writing Directors & Legal Writing Inst., 2005 Survey Results 11 (Question 20), 20 (Question 33), 21–22 (Question 35) (released July 2005) (available at http://www.alwd.org).

The Lessons of One Example

It's unrealistic to think that any one example could possibly reflect the manifold sins of traditional legal writing — or all the remedies. Advocates of plain language have argued long and hard for a flexible, expansive approach to change. We know that there is no one solution or one set of guidelines.

Still, some of the sins of legalese are committed with such confounded regularity that you just want to scream. How can lawyers be so stubborn or indifferent or unskilled? When will they start to change? Why can't they learn at least a few basic techniques? Learning and practicing even some of the plain-language techniques would go a long way toward improving the state of legal writing. And having made a start, many lawyers would catch the spirit and change their writing dramatically.

Below is a typical example, a 1975 Michigan statute — specifically, Michigan Compiled Law § 691.1502. It protects medical professionals who, like good Samaritans, voluntarily help someone in an emergency.

691.1502 Hospital or Other Medical Care Facility Personnel

(1) In instances where the actual hospital duty of that person did not require a response to that emergency situation, a physician, dentist, podiatrist, intern, resident, registered nurse, licensed practical nurse, registered physical therapist, clinical laboratory technologist, inhalation therapist, certified registered nurse anesthetist, x-ray technician, or paramedical person, who in good faith responds to a life threatening emergency or responds to a

145

request for emergency assistance in a life threatening emergency within a hospital or other licensed medical care facility, shall not be liable for any civil damages as a result of an act or omission in the rendering of emergency care, except an act or omission amounting to gross negligence or willful and wanton misconduct.

(2) The exemption from liability under subsection (1) shall not apply to a physician where a physician-patient relationship existed prior to the advent of the emergency nor to a licensed nurse where a nurse-patient relationship existed prior to the advent of the emergency.

(3) Nothing in this act shall diminish a hospital's responsibility to reasonably and adequately staff hospital emergency facilities when the hospital maintains or holds out to the general public that it maintains such emergency room facilities.

There are fundamental flaws here that can be remedied by plain language. Let's tick off some fixes.

- Break up the first sentence, which is way too long. Critics of plain language often argue that long sentences are not necessarily bad; they can be managed. But lawyers almost never manage them well. And that leads to related deficiencies.

- Close up the gap between the subject of the first sentence, all those medical persons, and the verb phrase, *shall not be liable*. (And get rid of *shall*. Make it *is not liable*.)

- Consider a more general way to describe the list of medical professionals. How can you be sure that you have listed every kind of professional? And what happens when a new kind of professional appears, as it surely will? My redraft below — which uses "a licensed or certified medical professional" — is obviously more general than the original is. And I'd say that it's not too vague. I realize, though, that the choices between general and specific language, and between vague and precise language, are perhaps the most difficult and controversial issues in drafting.

- Fix the two critical ambiguities in the middle of that long first sentence. The overload produces a syntactic ambiguity before and after the two possibilities in the middle of the sentence: "who in good faith responds to a life threatening emergency or responds to a request for emergency assistance in a life threatening emergency within a hospital or other licensed medical care facility." Ambiguity one: what does *in good faith* modify? Just the first *responds* or also the second *responds*? Ambiguity two: what does *within a hospital or other licensed medical care facility* modify? Just the second *life threatening emergency*? Or does it also modify the first *life threatening emergency*? In other words, is a doctor protected if he or she responds to a life-threatening emergency along the side of the road?

- Group related material together. Notice that the statute puts one exception at the end of subsection (1) and another in subsection (2).

- Use vertical lists.

- Get rid of inflated diction, like *prior to the advent of the emergency*.

- Use more headings.

Below is a possible redraft. I'm assuming that the "in good faith" requirement always applies. I'm also assuming that the statute does not apply to a doctor who stops to help along the road; that is, as the original title suggests, the statute applies only within a medical-care facility.

Immunity of Medical Professionals in an Emergency

(1) *Immunity for Responding to a Life-Threatening Emergency in a Hospital*

Under the following circumstances, a licensed or certified medical professional is not liable for civil damages that result from giving emergency care within a hospital or other licensed medical-care facility:

(a) the professional responds in good faith to a life-threatening emergency or to a request for assistance in a life-threatening emergency; and

(b) the professional's actual hospital duty [job responsibilities?] did not require him or her to respond.

(2) *Circumstances in Which the Immunity Does Not Apply*

This immunity does not apply in any of the following circumstances:

(a) the professional's conduct amounts to gross negligence or to willful and wanton misconduct.

(b) a physician who responds had a physician–patient relationship [with the treated person?] before the emergency; or

(c) a licensed nurse who responds had a nurse–patient relationship [with the treated person?] before the emergency.

(3) *A Hospital's Continuing Duty to Staff Its Emergency Facilities*

This act does not diminish a hospital's responsibility to properly staff its emergency facilities if the hospital maintains, or holds out to the public that it maintains, emergency-room facilities.

One last observation. In (1)(a), what is the point of specifying both of the "responds" possibilities — responds to an emergency and responds to a request for assistance in an emergency? Doesn't the first possibility swallow up the second? If we just said "responds in good faith to a life-threatening emergency," is there some danger that the statute might not be applied to a professional who responds to a request for assistance? I doubt it. In any event, this is exactly the kind of uncertainty and possible redundancy that plain-language drafting tends to expose. And even if we err on the side of certainty and precision, we don't have to sacrifice clarity. That may be the most important lesson of all.

∾ ∾ ∾

In 2002, after I wrote this article, the statute was amended to add another exception. At the same time, the first clause in (1) was changed to "If an individual's actual hospital duty does not require a response to the emergency situation." The misused *shall* in each section was changed to present tense — in (1), for instance, from *shall not be liable* to *is not liable*. In (2), *prior to the advent of the emergency* was changed to *before the emergency*. In (3), *Nothing in this act shall diminish* was changed to *This act does not diminish*, and *such* was omitted in *such emergency room facilities*. I don't claim any credit, but that's progress.

A Modest Wish List
for Legal Writing

The items on my wish list are not the most important things in life or the most important aspects of writing. They are some little ways to improve and to modernize legal writing.

I'm not going to provide authority for each of these points and subpoints. There is little dispute about them among experts on usage and style. If you'd like to see some authority, check the references in Appendix 2 to this book. You'll see a number of books by Bryan Garner — the Prosser of legal writing. It would be good to have all his books, but the one you must have is *A Dictionary of Modern Legal Usage* (2d ed. 1995). No lawyer should be without it — or argue legal style without consulting it.

Please note that the grammar program or spelling checker on your computer will turn up few, if any, of the items on my list. Technology can help to diagnose a limited number of stylistic flaws, but no amount of technology can create a good writer or a good piece of writing.

My wish list does have one premise: I'm assuming that you're more interested in being clear and readable than in sounding lawyerish.

1. Pay attention to how the page looks.

In the last 15 or 20 years, document designers have developed a set of guidelines for creating text that's both inviting and readable:

- Avoid all-capital letters. THEIR UNIFORM SIZE MAKES THEM NOTORIOUSLY HARD TO READ. Small letters have tops and tails that give them distinctive shapes.
- Avoid underlining. It's a hangover from the days of typewriters. To add emphasis, use italics or boldface.
- For text (as opposed to headings), prefer a serif typeface like Times New Roman or Garamond. Serifs are the little strokes (lines or curves) at the top and bottom of a letter.

> This is serif type (Garamond).
>
> This is sans-serif type (Arial).

Above all, avoid `Courier`.

- Use at least 12-point type, and never less than 10-point.
- Use left headings, not centered headings. Put them in boldface. Do not underline them. If you have subheadings, use a smaller-sized boldface or boldface italics.
- Use a ragged right margin unless the document is professionally typeset.
- Use lists and bullets. If the items have no rank order, prefer bullets.
- In lists and bullets, use hanging indents. That is, do not bring a second line back any farther than the first word in the first line.

2. Use sensible paragraphing and numbering.

When drafting rules, contracts, instructions, and the like, writers often create the long, dense paragraphs that drive readers crazy. Break these monsters down. Garner says that paragraphs — numbered parts or subparts — should average no more than 150 words.

The solution, of course, is to turn a long section into shorter sections or to create subsections. Occasionally, you may need a third level of breakdown — sub-subsections — but rarely more than that.

In numbering, avoid roman numerals and romanettes (like *iii*). They are too much like a foreign language.

You can distinguish different levels by using larger boldface for sections, smaller boldface for subsections, and italicized boldface for sub-subsections when needed. So a section (from a regulation requiring safety barriers around swimming pools) might look like this:

4. Requirements for Safety Barriers

   (A) Height

      (1) *Public Pools*

      . . .

      (2) *Private Pools*

      . . .

   (B) Location

With a modified decimal system, the same section would look like this:

4. Requirements for Safety Barriers

   4.1 Height

      (A) *Public Pools*

      . . .

      (B) *Private Pools*

      . . .

   4.2 Location

One advantage of the decimal system is that it simplifies the numbering. In the first example above, suppose you want to include a numbered list in 4(A)(1). You would probably have to list the items as (a), (b), and (c) to avoid repeating the parenthesized numbers. But with the decimal system, you can use (1), (2), (3).

Note that dividing a document into sections and subsections is different from creating a list within a sentence. But in both cases, you want to avoid extremes — either not enough levels of breakdown, or too many. Again, in dividing most documents, I would have no more than three levels (section, subsection, sub-subsection). In lists, I would have no more than two levels of breakdown. Federal statutes are gross offenders on both counts.

3. Let go of common superstitions.

All the experts scoff at the following "rules." They have no foundation in English grammar or style. Although some high-school teachers may still be under their spell, these supposed rules are just a bunch of old bogeys.

- Never end a sentence with a preposition. (Some writers are so spooked that they contort the *middle* of sentences: "To protect against the dangers about which he knew, the landlord fixed the loose railing.")
- Never split an infinitive. (If rhythm or clarity calls for a split, then split.)
- Never split a verb phrase. (In fact, adverbs usually follow an auxiliary verb: *will greatly increase*. With two auxiliary verbs, put the adverb after the first auxiliary unless the adverb and verb suggest an adjective and noun that could stand together: *will have greatly increased*. Here, *greatly increased* suggests "great increase.")
- Never begin a sentence with *And*, *But*, or *So*. (Listen to how you talk. *But* is far more common and more deft than *However* to show contrast at the beginning of a sentence. And when you start a sentence with one of these conjunctions, don't follow it with a comma; in that regard, they are different from *In addition*, *However*, and *Therefore*.)

- Never use contractions. (Maybe not in a brief, but why not in a letter or a law journal?)
- Never use *I* or *me*. (Use them unself-consciously. Avoid the genteel *myself* when you mean *I* or *me*.)
- Never refer to the reader as *you*. (On the contrary, *you* is invaluable for making consumer documents clear. It puts the reader directly into the picture.)

4. Avoid creating initialisms.

They may be trendy, but they are not clever or clear. They may save space, but they do not speed communication. They have become a menace to prose.

If you create an initialism or acronym — say, "Committee on Plain English (COPE)" — in one place and use it four paragraphs later, the reader will probably have forgotten what it stands for and have to look back. You can almost always find another shorthand, like *the committee*. For the "Elliott–Larsen Civil Rights Act," use *the act* or *the Elliott–Larsen Act* or *the Civil Rights Act* (not *ELCRA*). For "Thomas M. Cooley Law School," use *Thomas Cooley* or *Cooley* or *the school* (not *TMCLS*).

If an initialism has already entered the common vocabulary (*UAW*, *FBI*, *ADA*), fine; use it. But we should not be feverishly creating new ones at every opportunity. And we should certainly not have several different ones operating at once. Give words a chance.

By the way, nothing could be sillier than creating an initialism in one place and never using it again.

5. Shun the slash.

Apart from fractions and websites, the slash has almost no good uses. *And/or* is classic legalese. *S/he* is distracting, unpronounceable, and unnecessary; you can write in a gender-neutral style without resorting to typographical tricks. Instead of *alumni/ae*, how about *graduates*? Finally, use an en dash (the shorter dash), not a slash, to join equal or like terms: *landlord–tenant law, bench–bar conference, attorney–client relations, student–faculty ratio*. A hyphen is also acceptable.

6. Embrace the dash.

You can go for pages and pages in legal writing and never see a dash, probably because of the notion that dashes are somehow too informal for such a lofty enterprise. That's another bogey, and one that handicaps writers. Dashes are excellent for highlighting an inserted phrase — what Garner calls an interruptive phrase — within a sentence. They provide even more emphasis at the end of a sentence — when you want a kicker. Of course, like any other technique, they can be overdone.

7. Hyphenate phrasal adjectives.

On the first page of a recent issue of my school's newspaper, writers used the following phrases, all of which should have had hyphens but didn't:

- *new-class members* [do you see the difference between that and *new class members*?]
- *public-health education*
- *elective-course studies*
- *senior-year curriculum*
- *Michigan bar-examination performance*

Hyphens prevent reader miscues, even for half a second. *Michigan bar . . . and grill*? No. *Michigan bar-examination . . . performance*.

Do not use a hyphen, though, when one of these exceptions applies:

(1) the phrasal adjective contains an adverb that ends in *ly* followed by a past participle (*highly regarded authority*);

(2) the phrase follows the noun it modifies (*her paper was well written*);

(3) the phrase consists of a proper noun (*several New York cases*); or

(4) the phrase is a foreign phrase (*pro rata share*).

Because this point is such a hard sell, I offer some authority. The first quote is from Wilson Follett's *Modern American Usage* (1966 ed.); the second, from Garner's *The Winning Brief* (2d ed. 2004).

> The first and by far the greatest help to reading is the compulsory hyphening that makes a single adjective out of two words before a noun: *eighteenth-century painting/ fleet-footed Achilles/tumbled-down shack/Morse-code noises/single-stick expert*. Nothing gives away the incompetent amateur more quickly than the typescript that neglects this mark of punctuation ....

> Invariably, lawyers are skeptical of this point, as if it were something newfangled or alien. But professional editors learn this lesson early and learn it well: you need to hyphenate your phrasal adjectives.... Yet in working on briefs, I've had to contend with colleagues who wanted everything to be an exception. They have wanted to write the *no waiver of royalty clause*, and write it repeatedly. Meanwhile, others have wanted to refer to *the law of the case doctrine*. Unhyphenated, these phrases cause a slow style, full of double takes. And we lawyers ought to be doing better.

8. Avoid the quirks of newspaper style.

For the most part, newspaper style is clear and crisp. On a few points, though, it runs counter to the strong weight of authority and should be ignored. Not all newspapers exhibit these quirks, but most of them do.

First, newspapers don't use the serial comma. Most would write *Muddy Waters, Buddy Guy and Elmore James*. Put a comma after *Buddy Guy* to avoid possible ambiguity:

Muddy Waters, Buddy Guy, and Elmore James and the Broomdusters. Use the serial comma every time, without wondering whether you need it to avoid ambiguity.

Second, for singular nouns that end in *s*, newspapers form the possessive by adding an apostrophe, instead of *'s*: *Thomas' jump shot.* Make it *Thomas's jump shot.* After all, how do you pronounce it? Likewise, make it *a witness's testimony, Douglas's opinions, Congress's intent.*

Third, newspapers are fanatical about dropping the word *that* after verbs. More often than not, you need the conjunctive *that* after a verb to provide a joint in the sentence and prevent a possible miscue. But on the pages of most newspapers, you regularly find sentences made worse by the omission of *that.* Here is a sampling from one day's *Lansing State Journal*:

- The court ruled liability can exist only when school officials know about and are deliberately indifferent to sexual harassment.
- The court's four dissenters warned the ruling sets a dangerous precedent.
- Schauer admits concealed weapons isn't one of his favorite topics.
- State Board of Education President Dorothy Beardmore agreed too many changes are being thrown at schools.

A few verbs — *say, feel, think, hope* — will tolerate the omission of *that*, but most will not.

Fourth, newspapers overdo sentence fragments and one-sentence paragraphs. Both are especially beloved by sportswriters, perhaps on the theory that the gold medal goes to the breeziest style.

9. With numbers, avoid the quirks of legal style.

First, do not double up on words and numbers. Consider the following: "The redemption period shall be six (6) months from the date of sale unless the property is abandoned, in which case the redemption period shall be thirty (30) days from the date of sale." What, pray tell, is the point of the doubling? Is there any real chance of typographical error? Let's do it once and get it right. Otherwise, you produce monstrosities like this: "The amount claimed to be due on the mortgage is the sum of five hundred fifty-eight thousand two hundred ten and 23/ 100 dollars ($558,210.23)."

Second, generally use numerals for numbers above ten. In other words, forget *The Bluebook* on this one and join the rest of the world. Of course, there are special rules for money, measurements, fractions, and some others. *The Gregg Reference Manual* (10th ed. 2005) covers all the variations.

Third, do not show cents with round dollar figures. Write *a nonrefundable fee of $20* (not *$20.00*).

10. Prefer English plurals.

Over time, most foreign words become familiar enough that they lose their sense of foreignness and can take English plurals. We can argue over individual words, but given a fairly equal choice between alternatives, we should generally prefer English. Write *appendixes, formulas, forums, indexes, memorandums, millenniums, referendums, syllabuses, symposiums.*

On the other hand, some foreign plurals have not become anglicized: *analyses, bases, criteria, hypotheses, phenomena* (except for persons), *theses.* When in doubt, consult a good guide to current usage.

11. Give *shall* the boot; use *must* for required actions.

Nobody uses *shall* in ordinary speech. Nobody says, "You shall finish the project in a week." So unless lawyers can

make a case for *shall*, it should be relegated to the heap —
along with *aforesaid*, *to wit*, and all the rest.

Lawyers may argue that they use *shall* consistently to
impose a duty and that *shall* has a settled meaning in law.
Not true and not true.

Lawyers regularly misuse *shall* to mean something other
than "has a duty to":

- There shall be no right of appeal. [Change *shall be* to *is*.
  You are not imposing a duty; you are declaring a legal
  fact or policy.]

- "Days" shall be defined as calendar days, unless otherwise specified. [Change *shall be defined as* to *means*.
  Same reason as in the first example.]

- No professor or employee shall individually resolve or
  attempt to resolve a suspected violation. [Change *shall*
  to *may*. You are not negating a duty; you are negating
  permission.]

- Appropriate sanctions shall include any one or more of
  the following . . . . [Omit *shall*. Better yet, identify the
  agent. If you are imposing a duty, make it *The hearing
  panel must impose one or more of the following sanctions*. If you are granting permission, make it *The hearing
  panel may impose one or more of the following sanctions*.]

Shall has become so corrupted by misuse that it has no
firm meaning. It can mean "must," "should," "will," "may,"
or "is." No wonder, then, that *Words and Phrases* takes 104
pages to summarize the more than 1,300 cases interpreting
shall.

Since *must* is less legalistic and less corrupted, it's a better
choice for required actions, and the change has already
started to take place. The new Federal Rules of Appellate
and Criminal Procedure, for instance, use *must*, not *shall*.
So do the proposed new Federal Rules of Civil Procedure.

12. Banish *prior to.*

Prior to takes the booby prize for the most common inflated phrase in legal and official writing. Why would anyone prefer it to *before*? Try to think of a single literary title or line that uses *prior to*. " 'Twas the night prior to Christmas"? "The land was ours prior to our having been the land's"? "And miles to go prior to my sleeping"?

By itself, *prior to* may seem insignificant, but it often leads to clunky wording:

- prior to the commencement of the hearing [*before the hearing begins*].

- prior to the service upon the defendant of the plaintiff's motion [*before the plaintiff's motion is served on the defendant*].

- prior to the time when a decision is filed [*before the court files a decision*].

More important, a fondness for *prior to* may indicate a fondness for jargon — and a blind resistance to using plain words. That resistance, that cast of mind, is in large part responsible for the state of legal writing.

Plain Words

I write this article — and offer the four lists below — with some trepidation. I will be accused of promoting baby talk, of constricting and dumbing down the language, of denying writers their expressive voice, and of corrupting legal discourse. That's the fate of anyone who believes that lawyers should write in a plainer style.

I have tried to address these false charges — these myths about plain language — in other articles. For now, I'll settle for just a few reminders about my list.

First, it deals with the choice of words. And vocabulary is just one part of plain language. Plain language, rightly understood, involves all the techniques for clear communication: planning the document, designing it, organizing it, constructing sentences, choosing words, and testing mass documents on typical readers.

Second, plain language has nothing against expressiveness in a brief, for instance, or a mediation summary. But literary flair has little or no place in statutes, rules, contracts, wills and trusts, forms, and most pleadings. Besides, the words on the left below, under "Instead of," are not so fresh or forceful that they might create a pleasing effect.

Third, some of those words are more stodgy than others, and we could argue about where each one falls along the line from "not so bad" to "never use." (I'd rather take a kick in the shins than use *cognizant of* or *requisite* or *utilize*, for instance.) Every writer has to make these choices, always with the audience and context in mind.

Fourth, the choice of words may depend on more than just simplicity. It may depend on the rhythm or sound of the sentence. And, of course, the choice may depend on precision. By all means, use the longer, less familiar word if you think it's more precise or accurate. When in doubt, check a book on usage or a dictionary that discriminates between synonyms.[1]

Finally, your readers will not notice an occasional big word. But they will notice — even unconsciously — a tendency toward inflated diction, and they will not be impressed or persuaded.

The great H.W. Fowler got it right almost 100 years ago:

> Prefer the familiar word to the far-fetched.
> Prefer the concrete word to the abstraction.
> Prefer the single word to the circumlocution.
> Prefer the short word to the long.
> Prefer the Saxon word to the Romance.[2]

In my high-school English class (before English became "Language Arts"), we had to learn ten vocabulary words each week. It occurred to me that I might be rewarded for sprinkling these words like salt on my papers. So in one essay, I did just that. When it came back, there were two words on the cover: "turgid, inflated." Grade: C–.

Remember what Fowler said. And remember what George Bernard Shaw said: "In literature the ambition of a novice is to acquire the literary language; the struggle of the adept is to get rid of it."[3]

---

[1] *E.g.*, Theodore M. Bernstein, *The Careful Writer* (1965); Roy H. Copperud, *American Usage and Style: The Consensus* (1980); Bryan A. Garner, *Garner's Modern American Usage* (2d ed. 2003); Bryan A. Garner, *A Dictionary of Modern Legal Usage* (2d ed. 1995); *Funk & Wagnalls Modern Guide to Synonyms* (S.I. Hayakawa ed., 1968); *Webster's New Dictionary of Synonyms* (1973).

[2] H.W. Fowler & F.G. Fowler, *The King's English* 11 (1906; 3d ed. 1931).

[3] Quoted in John R. Trimble, *Writing with Style* 183 (2d ed. 2000).

Instead of	Consider
accede to	grant, allow
accompany	go with
accomplish	do, achieve
accordingly	so, therefore
accumulate	gather, get, have
additional	more, added, other
additionally	and, also
adjacent to	close to, near, next to
administer	manage
advantageous	useful, helpful
advise	tell, recommend
afford	give
aggregate	total
allocate	give, divide, set aside
alter	change
alteration	change
alternative	other, other choice
anticipate	expect
append	attach
apprise	tell, inform
approximately	about, almost, roughly
ascertain	find out, learn, determine
assist	help
assistance	help
attain	reach, become
attempt (verb)	try
biannually	twice a year
calculate	work out, figure
category	kind, class, group
cease	end, stop
cognizant of	aware of, know
commence	begin, start
commencement	beginning, start
commitment	promise
communicate	write, tell, talk
compensation	pay, payment
complete (verb)	finish, fill out

Instead of	Consider
comply with	follow, meet
component	part
comprise	consist of, contain
conceal	hide
concept	idea
concerning	about, on, for
concur	agree
consequence	result
consequently	so, therefore
consolidate	combine, join
constitute	make up
construct	build, make
contiguous to	next to, bordering on
customary	usual
decrease (verb)	reduce, lower
deem	consider, think, treat as
defer	delay, put off
demise	death
demonstrate	show, prove
depart	go, leave
designate	appoint, name, choose, set
desire	wish, want
desist	stop
detain	hold
diminish	lessen, reduce
discontinue	stop
disseminate	send out, distribute
donate	give
duration	time, rest
effectuate	carry out, bring about
elapse	pass
elucidate	explain, clarify
employ	use
employment	work, job
encounter (verb)	meet, face, run into
endeavor (verb)	try

Instead of	Consider
ensure	make sure
[is] entitled to	has a right to
enumerate	list, name
equivalent	equal, the same
evince	show
exclude	leave out
exhibit (verb)	have, show
expedite	hasten, speed up
expend	spend
expenditure	payment, expense, cost
expiration	end
facilitate	make easier, help
following (preposition)	after
formulate	work out, devise
forward (verb)	send
frequently	often
furnish	give, provide
hence	so, therefore
however	but
identical	same
illustrate	show
impact (verb)	affect, influence
implement	carry out, begin, start, create, set up
inception	start, beginning
indicate	say, show, suggest
indication	sign
individual (noun)	person
inform	tell
initial	first
initiate	begin, start, set up
inquire	ask
institute	begin, start, set up
interrogate	question
locate	find, place
magnitude	size
maintain	keep, continue, support
manner	way

Instead of	Consider
maximum	most, largest, greatest
modification	change
modify	change
necessitate	require
necessity	need, requirement
notification	notice
notwithstanding	despite
numerous	many
objective (noun)	goal, aim
obligate	bind, compel, require
obligation	debt, duty, responsibility
observe	see, watch, follow, obey
obtain	get
obviate	avoid
occasion (verb)	cause
occur	happen
ongoing	continuing, active
opt for	choose
optimum	best
option	choice
parameter	limit, boundary, guideline, condition
participate	take part
per annum	a year
personnel	people, staff
peruse	read with care, review
per year	a year
place (verb)	put
portion	part
possess	have, own
preclude	prevent
preferable	best, better, preferred
premises	place, property
prescribed	set, required
present (verb)	give
previous	earlier, last, past
previously	before, earlier

Instead of	Consider
principal	main, chief
prior	earlier
proceed	go, go ahead
procure	buy, get
promulgate	make, issue, pass
provide	give, send
provided that	if, but
purchase (verb)	buy
pursuant to	under
receive	get
regarding	about, on, for
reimburse	repay, pay back
remainder	rest
render	make, give
represents	is, makes up, stands for
request (verb)	ask
requisite (adjective)	needed, required
reside	live
respond	answer, reply
responsible for	causes, has charge of
retain	keep
selection	choice
semiannually	twice a year
similar to	like
solely	only
specified	named, set out
submit	send, offer
subsequent	later
subsequently	later, afterward, then
sufficient	enough
summon	send for, call
terminate	end, stop
thus	so
transmit	send
transpire	happen
utilize	use
visualize	think of, imagine

Next are two lists of wordy phrases. The first list separates out multiword prepositions (also called compound or complex or phrasal prepositions). You'll notice how many of them end in *of*, and you'll sense how pervasive they are. Writing about compound prepositions in his classic *Dictionary of Modern English Usage*, Fowler said that, while some are worse than others, "taken as a whole, they are almost the worst element in modern English, stuffing up what is written with a compost of nouny abstractions."[5]

The cure is at hand. Almost always, you can replace the wordy phrases on the left.

Multiword Prepositions	Shorter, Simpler
as a means of	to
as to	on, for, about, of
by means of	by, with
by reason of	because of
by virtue of	by, under, because of
during the period from	from
for a period of	for
from the point of view of	from, for
in addition to	besides
in back of	behind
in connection with	with, about, concerning, for
in excess of	more than, over
in favor of	for
in lieu of	instead of, rather than
[be] in receipt of	have
in terms of	in, for, about
in the absence of	without
in the amount of	for
in the case of	in, with (or cut it)
in the nature of	like
in the neighborhood of	about, roughly
on behalf of	for

5 *A Dictionary of Modern English Usage* 102 (Ernest Gowers ed., 2d ed. 1965).

Multiword Prepositions	Shorter, Simpler
on the basis of	by, from, because of
on the occasion of	on
on the part of	by, for
under the provisions of	under
with the exception of	except for

(Grouped by meaning)

as regards	about, concerning,
in reference to	on, for
in regard to	
in relation to	
with reference to	
with regard to	
with respect to	
concerning the matter of	
as a consequence of	because of, from
as a result of	
prior to	before
previous to	
antecedent to	
anterior to	
subsequent to	after
posterior to	
in the course of	during
during the course of	
in proximity to	close to, near
in the vicinity of	
for the purpose of	to, for
in order to	
with a view to	
with the object of	

Other Wordy Phrases	Shorter, Simpler
in the event that	if, when
in a situation where	
under circumstances in which	

Other Wordy Phrases	Shorter, Simpler
due to the fact that because of the fact that in view of the fact that for the reason that inasmuch as	because, since, given that
despite the fact that notwithstanding the fact that	although, even though
during such time as during the time that	while
at present at the present time at this point in time	now, currently
at an early date in the near future	soon
at the time that at such time as	when
at the place where in the place in which	where
until such time as	until
it is [necessary, important] that	must, should
has discretion to is permitted to is authorized to	may
is able to is in a position to has the ability to	can
there is no doubt but that	doubtless, no doubt
this is a [topic, subject] that	this topic
the question as to whether	whether, the question whether
it would appear that	apparently
it is probable that	probably

Other Wordy Phrases	Shorter, Simpler
in a [negligent, precise] manner	negligently, precisely
on a daily basis	daily, every day
a large [number, percentage] of	many
the majority of	most
sufficient number of adequate number of	enough
excessive number of	too many
have a negative impact	hurt, harm
no later than June 30 on or before June 30	before July 1

We come finally to the lawyerisms — words and formalisms that give legal writing its musty smell. They should be completely avoided. Total abstinence. Either cut them entirely or find a plain, modern-day equivalent.

This is not a complete list, but it includes many of the most common offenders.

ab initio
above-mentioned
ad idem
aforementioned
aforesaid
anent
arguendo
before-mentioned
below-mentioned
case at bar
ex contractu
ex delicto
foregoing
Further affiant
  sayeth naught

henceforth
hereafter
hereby
herein
hereinafter
hereinbefore
hereof
heretofore
hereunto
herewith
instant case,
  matter, etc.
instanter
inter alia
inter se

In Witness
  Whereof
Know All Men by
  These Presents
Now comes the
  plaintiff
premises (in the
  sense of "matters
  already referred
  to")
said (for *the*, *that*,
  or *those*)
same (for *it* or
  them)
ss.

sub judice	therewith	wherein
such (for *the*, *that*, etc.)	to wit	whereof
	unto	wheresoever
thenceforth	vel non	whosoever
thereafter	viz.	within-named
thereat	whatsoever	witnesseth
therefor	whensoever	(and other
therein	whereat	verbs ending
thereof	Wherefore,	in -*eth*)
thereunto	defendant prays	

Go forth and simplify.

A Litany of Complaints

"I would wish that the superfluous and tedious statutes were brought into one sum together and made more plain and short so that men might better understand them."

King Edward VI (1537–1553)
(as quoted in Jim Kennan, *The Importance of Plain English in Drafting*,
in *Essays on Legislative Drafting* 74, 78
(David St. L. Kelly ed., Adelaide L. Rev. Assn. 1988))

"[T]o speak effectually, plainly, and shortly, it becometh the gravity of this profession."

Sir Edward Coke (1552–1634),
Reports of Sir Edward Coke vol. 2, xlii
(John Henry Thomas & John Farquhar Fraser eds., 1826)

"[T]his Society [of lawyers] hath a peculiar Cant and Jargon of their own, that no other Mortal can understand, and wherein all their Laws are written, which they take special Care to multiply; whereby they have wholly confounded the very Essence of Truth and Falsehood, of Right and Wrong; so that it will take Thirty Years to decide whether the Field, left me by my Ancestors for six Generations, belong to me, or to a Stranger three Hundred Miles off."

Jonathan Swift, *Gulliver's Travels* 203 (1726)
(Ricardo Quintana ed., Modern Lib. 1958)

"[I]t would be useful . . . to reform the style of [American statutes,] which, from their verbosity, their endless tautologies, . . . and their multiplied efforts at certainty, by *saids* and *aforesaids*, by *ors* and by *ands*, to make them more plain, are really rendered more perplexed and incomprehensible, not only to common readers, but to the lawyers themselves."

> Thomas Jefferson (1743–1826),
> *The Writings of Thomas Jefferson* vol. 1, 65
> (Andrew A. Lipscomb ed., 1904)

"In its style [a bill on criminal law], I have aimed at accuracy, brevity, and simplicity, preserving, however, the very words of the established law, wherever their meaning had been sanctioned by judicial decisions, or rendered technical by usage. The same matter, if couched in the modern statutory language, with all its tautologies, redundancies, and circumlocutions, would have spread itself over many pages, and been unintelligible to those whom it most concerns. Indeed, I wished to exhibit a sample of reformation in the barbarous style into which modern statutes have degenerated from their ancient simplicity."

> Thomas Jefferson (1743–1826),
> *The Writings of Thomas Jefferson*
> vol. 1, app., note E, 216
> (Andrew A. Lipscomb ed., 1904)

"For this redundancy — for the accumulation of excrementitious matter in all its various shapes . . . — for all the pestilential effects that cannot but be produced by this so enormous a load of literary garbage, — the plea commonly pleaded . . . is, that it is necessary to *precision* — or, to use the word which on similar occasions [drafters] themselves are in the habit of using, *certainty*. But a more absolutely sham plea never was . . . pleaded . . . ."

> Jeremy Bentham (1748–1832),
> *The Works of Jeremy Bentham* vol. 3, 260
> (John Bowring ed., ca. 1843; repr. 1962)

"[T]here is one abuse, against which I would especially caution you, because it is the least pardonable of all. I refer to the unconscionable redundancy of all legal instruments and proceedings. . . . [L]awyers, because in former times they were paid by the letter, have aimed to make their forms as long and incomprehensible as possible; and they too have admirably succeeded. The fictions, tautologies, and circumlocutions devised by them to elongate legal documents, may be cited as specimens of marvelous ingenuity. . . . The evil may seem trivial in a single case; but when you take into view all the legal forms, and the millions who daily use them, the aggregate swells into an enormous magnitude."

Timothy Walker, *Advice to Law Students*,
1 Western L.J. 481, 485 (1844)

"On such an afternoon, some score of members of the High Court of Chancery bar . . . are . . . mistily engaged in one of the ten thousand stages of an endless cause, tripping one another up on slippery precedents, groping knee-deep in technicalities, running their goat-hair and horse-hair warded heads against walls of words, and making a pretence of equity with serious faces, as players might."

Charles Dickens, *Bleak House* 6 (1852–1853)
(George Ford & Sylvère Monod eds., W.W. Norton & Co. 1977)

"In the heels of the higgling lawyers, Bob,
Too many slippery ifs and buts and howevers,
Too much hereinbefore provided whereas,
Too many doors to go in and out of."

Carl Sandburg, from the poem
"The Lawyers Know Too Much" (1920)

"There are two things wrong with almost all legal writing. One is its style. The other is its content. That, I think, about covers the ground."

Fred Rodell, *Goodbye to Law Reviews*,
23 Va. L. Rev. 38, 38 (1936)

"It strikes everyone as an extreme case of the evils of jargon when a man is tried by a law he can't read, in a court which uses a language he can't understand."

A.P. Rossiter, *Our Living Language* 86 (1953)

"Almost all legal sentences . . . have a way of reading as though they had been translated from the German by someone with a rather meager knowledge of English. Invariably they are long. Invariably they are awkward. Invariably and inevitably they make plentiful use of . . . abstract, fuzzy, clumsy words . . . ."

Fred Rodell, *Woe Unto You, Lawyers!* 124–25
(rev. ed. 1957; repr. 1987)

"The language of the law has a strong tendency to be wordy, unclear, pompous, and dull."

David Mellinkoff, *The Language of the Law* 24 (1963)

"[L]egalese is worse than smoking cigarettes. To kick the habit is extremely hard. So don't kid yourself. If you want to write plain English, you'll have to learn how. You'll have to study it as if it were Spanish or French. It'll take much work and lots of practice until you've mastered the skill."

Rudolf Flesch, *How to Write Plain English:
A Book for Lawyers and Consumers* 2 (1979)

"Lawyers have two common failings. One is that they do not write well and the other is that they think they do."

Carl Felsenfeld, *The Plain English Movement in the United States*,
6 Canadian Business L.J. 408, 413 (1981–1982)

"Something strange happens when human beings enter law school. Perfectly normal, usually intelligent, and relatively sophisticated people begin what can only be described as a process of intellectual brainwashing. Few who are exposed ever recover. . . . Soon after entering law school [students] get the notion that to be lawyers, they must learn to speak and write like lawyers. The straightforward language that has gotten them through life up to then no longer issues from their lips."

Ronald L. Goldfarb & James C. Raymond,
Clear Understandings: A Guide to Legal Writing 3 (1982)

"Brief-writing runs from abysmal to mediocre. About 10 percent of the briefs I read are briefs that really show professional skill at written communications."

Ruggero J. Aldisert (as quoted in Charlotte Low Allen,
Skilled Legal Writing Becomes Exceptional,
5 Insight on the News 50 (Dec. 25, 1989–Jan. 1, 1990))

"[Lawbooks are] the largest body of poorly written literature ever created by the human race."

John M. Lindsey, *The Legal Writing Malady:
Causes and Cures*, 204 N.Y. L.J. 2 (Dec. 12, 1990)

"The fact is that legal writing, as it pours out of thousands of word-processors, is overblown yet timid, homogeneous, and swaddled in obscurity. The legal academy is positively inimical to spare, decent writing."

Lawrence M. Friedman, *How I Write*,
4 Scribes J. Legal Writing 3, 5 (1993)

"For a hundred years, good lawyers have been writing without all the garbage and in a simple, direct style."

Lynn N. Hughes (as quoted in Bryan A. Garner,
Judges on Effective Writing: The Importance of Plain Language,
73 Mich. B.J. 326, 326 (1994))

"When it comes to plain talk, lawyers are the worst. Most speak and write as if they live in a repository for dead bodies. When they write briefs that some poor trapped judge must read, they fill them with heavy, gray, lifeless, disgustingly boring word gravel — piles of it, tons of it. When I read most briefs I want to scream. I want to throw the brief out the window and jump. If I could find the author, and had the power, I would make the villain eat the thing a page at a time without salt or catsup."

Gerry Spence, *How to Argue and Win Every Time* 104–05 (1995)

"[W]e [lawyers] have a history of wretched writing, a history that reinforces itself every time we open the lawbooks."

Bryan A. Garner, *The Elements of Legal Style* 2 (2d ed. 2002)

"Most lawyers write poorly. That's not just our lament. Leading lawyers across the country agree [according to a survey]. They think modern legal writing is flabby, prolix, obscure, opaque, ungrammatical, dull, boring, redundant, disorganized, gray, dense, unimaginative, impersonal, foggy, infirm, indistinct, stilted, arcane, confused, heavy-handed, jargon- and cliché-ridden, ponderous, weaseling, overblown, pseudointellectual, hyperbolic, misleading, incivil, labored, bloodless, vacuous, evasive, pretentious, convoluted, rambling, incoherent, choked, archaic, orotund, and fuzzy."

Tom Goldstein & Jethro K. Lieberman,
The Lawyer's Guide to Writing Well 3 (2d ed. 2002)

"We lawyers do not write plain English. We use eight words to say what could be said in two. We use arcane phrases to express commonplace ideas. Seeking to be precise, we become redundant. Seeking to be cautious, we become verbose. Our sentences twist on, phrase within clause within clause, glazing the eyes and numbing the minds of our readers."

Richard C. Wydick, *Plain English for Lawyers* 3 (5th ed. 2005)

APPENDIX 2

A Plain-Language Bookshelf

Four Indispensable Guides to Usage and Style

- Bryan A. Garner, *A Dictionary of Modern Legal Usage* (2d ed., Oxford U. Press 1995).

- Bryan A. Garner, *Garner's Modern American Usage* (2d ed., Oxford U. Press 2003).

- Bryan A. Garner, *The Redbook: A Manual on Legal Style* (West 2002).

- William A. Sabin, *The Gregg Reference Manual* (10th ed., McGraw–Hill 2005).

Books on Plain Writing

- Mark Adler, *Clarity for Lawyers* (2d ed., The Law Society of England 2006).

- Irwin Alterman, *Plain and Accurate Style in Court Papers* (ALI–ABA 1987).

- Michèle M. Asprey, *Plain Language for Lawyers* (3d ed., The Fedn. Press 2003).

- Jacques Barzun, *Simple & Direct: A Rhetoric for Writers* (rev. ed., Harper & Row 1985).

- Peter Butt & Richard Castle, *Modern Legal Drafting* (Cambridge U. Press 2001).

- Martin Cutts, *Clarifying Eurolaw* (Plain Lang. Commn. 2001).

- Martin Cutts, *Lucid Law* (2d ed., Plain Lang. Commn. 2000).

- Martin Cutts, *Oxford Guide to Plain English* (Oxford U. Press 2004).

- Robert C. Dick, *Legal Drafting in Plain English* (3d ed., Carswell 1995).

- Robert D. Eagleson, *Writing in Plain English* (Australian Govt. Printing Serv. 1990).

- Carl Felsenfeld & Alan Siegel, *Writing Contracts in Plain English* (West 1981).

- Rudolf Flesch, *How to Write Plain English: A Book for Lawyers and Consumers* (Harper & Row 1979).

- Bryan A. Garner, *The Elements of Legal Style* (2d ed., Oxford U. Press 2002).

- Bryan A. Garner, *Guidelines for Drafting and Editing Court Rules* (Admin. Off. U.S. Courts 1996).

- Bryan A. Garner, *Legal Writing in Plain English* (U. Chicago Press 2001).

- Bryan A. Garner, *The Winning Brief* (2d ed., Oxford U. Press 2004).

- Tom Goldstein & Jethro K. Lieberman, *The Lawyer's Guide to Writing Well* (2d ed., U. California Press 2002).

- Ernest Gowers, *The Complete Plain Words* (Sidney Greenbaum & Janet Whitcut eds., 3d ed., David R. Godine 1988).

- Christine Mowat, *A Plain Language Handbook for Legal Writers* (Carswell 1998).

- Thomas A. Murawski, *Writing Readable Regulations* (Carolina Acad. Press 1999).

- Mark Painter, *The Legal Writer* (3d ed., Jarndyce & Jarndyce Press 2005).

- Plain English Campaign, *Language on Trial: The Plain English Guide to Legal Writing* (1996).

- Plain English Campaign, *The Plain English Story* (3d rev. ed. 1993).

- Janice C. Redish, *How to Write Regulations and Other Legal Documents in Clear English* (Am. Insts. for Research 1991).

- Wayne Schiess, *Writing for the Legal Audience* (Carolina Acad. Press 2003).

- U.S. Securities and Exchange Commission, *A Plain English Handbook*, available at http://www.sec.gov/pdf/handbook.pdf.

- Richard C. Wydick, *Plain English for Lawyers* (5th ed., Carolina Acad. Press 2005).

Two Valuable Journals

- *Clarity*, published by Clarity, the international association promoting plain legal language. See www.clarity-international.net.

- *The Scribes Journal of Legal Writing*, published by Scribes — The American Society of Writers on Legal Subjects. See www.scribes.org.

ACKNOWLEDGMENTS

The list below shows where the essays in this book were first published:

- *The Straight Skinny on Better Judicial Opinions* and *How to Mangle Court Rules and Jury Instructions* — in *The Scribes Journal of Legal Writing*.
- *The Great Myth That Plain Language Is Not Precise* — in *Business Law Today*.
- *First Things First: The Lost Art of Summarizing*, *How to Write an Impeachment Order*, and *A Crack at Federal Drafting* — in *Court Review*.
- *The Lessons of One Example* — in *Clarity*.
- *A Modest Wish List for Legal Writing* and *Plain Words* — in *Trial*. Copyright The Association of Trial Lawyers of America.
- All others — in the *Michigan Bar Journal*.

INDEX